overcoming writer's block

THE WRITER'S GUIDE TO BEATING THE BLANK PAGE

MARCY PUSEY

Published by Miramare Ponte Press, LLC

Cover design by Danijela Mijailovic

e-book ISBN-13: 978-1-948283-23-6
Paperback ISBN-13: 978-1-948283-24-3
Hardback ISBN-13: 978-1-948283-25-0
Library of Congress Control Number: 2022948241

I'd love to give you a free guide to publishing, all the way from writing your book through post-launch tips. Gathered from hundreds of publishing experiences as a publishing press as well as an award-winning author. Grab it free!

Do you want the guide for children's authors? Grab it here: miramarepontepress.com/publish

contents

To every writer who's ever struggled to get to the finish line—

Your story is worth it.

You are worth it.

Keep going.

—M.P.

"Confront the page that taunts you with its whiteness. Face your enemy and fill it with words. You are bigger and stronger than a piece of paper."

—Fennel Hudson

introduction

Have you ever stared at a blank page feeling stuck and uninspired... or worse, like an imposter? Or maybe you *know* the words you want to write but just... don't? Welcome to the author's journey! While some authors will never move beyond the blinking cursor, stick with me and *you will.*

Writer's block is everywhere. Books, articles, and even TED talks attempt to address this seeming monster that pervades our homes and offices. The foreshocks of writer's block are enough to debilitate any aspiring writer. Frozen in our seats, we stare at the blinking cursor and blank page, dumbfounded. Our minds flood with all of the reasons we are uninspired... *Am I fooling myself? Who am I to write a book? I can't do this. How will I finish an entire manuscript when I can't get past this one page? I suck, everything sucks, I should quit.* The deafening silence of writer's block makes space for all of our insecurities, fears, and discomfort to face us full-on.

In this book, I will show you what writer's block *really is,* address the neurology of the blockage, and discuss strategies for moving through and beyond it with ease.

I'm going to show you how to be storm-prepared for writer's block. You'll get actual tips and strategies for outsmarting the giant when it comes knocking on your door. I'm going to help you understand the causes of writer's block so you can take your "vitamins" to keep you out of the writer's block ER. By the time you're done with this book, you'll be fully equipped to address any effort of writer's block to derail you.

How can I say this so confidently? Well, I'm a writer. I've had to face my demons so. many. times. Shoot, even getting started on *this* book (oh, the irony) has forced me to take my own advice and keep moving forward. This is my nineteenth book. I wish I could say the potential for writer's block goes away after a while—but no. It just becomes more recognizable. But as you learn more about *yourself*, how you're uniquely wired, and how to optimize that for your writing journey, you'll be able to flick writer's block off your shoulder like the pansy piece of lint that it is.

So many gurus in the world want to convince you that their *one way* to conquering writer's block is the *only* way. I don't believe that. As we look into who *you* are, you'll begin to see why someone else's strategy hasn't, and shouldn't, work for you, and instead, find the one that does. That's my approach to this book... not to tell you, "This is my way so it's also *your way*." Instead, I hope to open your eyes and heart to the possible reasons *you*, unique *you*, get stuck. Fortunately, there are some patterns we can look at to narrow down what does or doesn't work for you. Ultimately, this is a book of resources that you can pull from. Use what works for you.

I've coached *hundreds* of authors through the years in story development, writing, and publishing. I've heard just as many reasons why people get stuck. And I've helped all of them get UNstuck. It's my jam. I have a knack for getting beneath the superficial reasons (usually, "I don't have time, money, or the knowledge.") to the *real* reason. This might be my education in therapy (I'm a Certified Trauma and Resilience Practitioner) and how I've geeked out studying the brain.

It might be how *I'm* wired—to help others dig deep and get set free. In any case, I'm giving you my years of experience helping others break free so you can break free too.

Throughout this book, I'll share a number of real-life stories of people I've worked with and the obstacles they overcame with some coaching and willingness to look a little deeper. You can check out many of their published books here at miramarepontepress.com/authors-weve-worked-with.

This is not an exhaustive list, but it includes a lot of the authors I've worked with as an editor or done-for-you/done-with-you publisher. I can't help but hold each of their books and see the faces and hear the stories of the author behind them. I had a front-row seat to every one of their journeys. We laughed together, cried together, and celebrated together. I watched these authors overcome incredible odds, get knocked down and get back up again, wrestle with themselves and their stories... they did the hard work, and it makes me *beam* with pride. Not my own, but on their behalf. The author journey is incredibly beautiful, but it's not without a hard-fought battle.

A couple of them have passed away now, and I hold their books and cry in gratitude that their legacy outlives them. One passed away in the middle of her third book, so now I'm helping her adult children finish it. Not even death can keep her book from sitting in the hands of children.

Every single one of these authors got stuck at one point or another. All of them stared at a blank page. Some of them even quit for *years.* Like, one of my authors refused to give up for thirty years. She's finally publishing it this year. Why? Because her story matters and it wouldn't let her go. She got some coaching, accountability, and my publishing services... and that changed everything.

Stick with me and you *will* know how to attack every threat of writer's block. Never stare at another blank page again.

I mean, unless you want to. It really *is* a choice. Some people don't want to put in the work of preparing for a writer's block battle. They want easy, smooth, and pain-free. Unfortunately, avoiding pain will only cause more of it. These are the people who will die without their book on shelves to outlive them. These are the people who will live their lives believing the lie that they weren't good enough, skilled enough, important enough, or capable enough to get their message into the world. They'll die "small" having missed one of their greatest life callings—to tell their story.

Imagine if Brené Brown had given in to her own fears and insecurities and kept her messages from the world? How many people would have continued living in shame and isolation in her fear-induced silence? Some authors leave people stuck in their pain by withholding their message.

But that's not you. You've picked up this book because you don't want to be that person. You don't want to die with your legacy alone in your heart. You don't want to leave the world around you hurting a single day longer. You don't want to lie on your deathbed wondering if your life had any meaning.

It does. And you know it. So, let's get your message into the world. You don't have to fight the obstacles alone. Let's do this.

"Writer's block is just a symptom of feeling like you have nothing to say, combined with the rather weird idea that you should feel the need to say something. Why? If you have something to say, then say it. If not, enjoy the silence while it lasts. The noise will return soon enough."

—Hugh MacLeod

CHAPTER ONE

your story matters

In my experience, one of the foundational causes for people getting stuck is not believing that their story really matters.

"But there are already so many books out there."

"I'm just little ol' normal, insignificant me. What do I have to say that will help anyone?"

"I haven't *arrived* so how can I help anyone? I still struggle..."

Yet each of these people has a nudging that keeps pestering them, a compulsion to *tell their story*. Why? Because it *does* matter!

Unfortunately (but fortunately), "Your Story Matters" is trending. This is unfortunate because we begin to take it less seriously. It's fortunate because it's true! We need the reminder.

Are there already too many books on forgiveness in the world? Well, look around—does it look like the world has figured out forgiveness? No? Then let's keep putting stories out there. Your story matters.

Are you just a little ol' insignificant you? Well, guess what? That's 99.9 percent of the world, which makes you super relatable and relevant. Your story matters.

Oh, you still struggle with the things you want to help people with? Depression? Money management? Learning how to write a good story? Great! Then the struggle is *fresh.* You aren't too far removed from the pain of the journey to have forgotten what people are going through. Write from the struggle and share what you've learned along the way. Your story matters.

I don't even need to meet you to know the world needs your story, whether it's fiction or non fiction. I'm a firm, confident, committed believer in the power of your unique message, your personal journey with your story, and the many people out there who need *your* voice to take the next step in their own life.

Here's something else I've noticed. *Years* ago, we all cared about someone's credentials. "Oh, he's a PhD? Then I fully trust everything he's saying." Bwahahahahaha. Can you imagine putting your trust in someone *today* because of the letters after their name? There's been a pivot from credibility being one's level of education or social status to, "But have you walked in my shoes?" Readers most want to know if you *get them.* Can you relate to *their* struggle? We've grown tired of people giving us textbook answers with no real-life change. We want what *works* from someone who's tried it. Am I right? I'm right.

You, living your life, struggling through your struggles, and getting out of bed day after day is credibility. Your grit is credibility. Your failures are credibility (as long as you don't stay there). Your humanity is credibility.

So yes, we need your story.

Here's another list of reasons we need your story, each of which I'll dig into deeper in the upcoming chapters. Because while these are reasons we need your story, they can also become obstacles to getting your story into the world.

- Neurologically, *your brain heals* when you engage with, wrestle with, and share your story. If for no other reason than your own freedom and health, your story matters.
- When your story just *isn't* coming out, for the page, the stage, or a friend—it's not because it doesn't matter. It's the opposite—it matters SO much that it still needs you to wrestle with it. Once you've made enough peace with it, it will come out. Your story matters.
- When you share your story, and other humans receive it, you are CHANGING *THEIR* BRAIN. You have the power (and thus responsibility) to put your story into the world for the growth and healing of others. Your story matters.
- When you share stories of overcoming *any* obstacle, you leave hope and inspiration in the lives of others. You help our community strengthen and believe in possibility. Your story matters.
- When you share your story, in your voice, your style, and your particular experience, you reach an entire group of people who just couldn't connect with other stories and storytellers. Friends, they're waiting on YOU. Your story matters.

This is not exhaustive. But if you need a million more reasons, I'll give them to you. I have been changed by the stories of insecure, "insignificant," fearful people. Because they were brave and did it anyway. I'm indebted to every scared voice that lifted for my sake. I will champion every voice that might do the same for someone else until I'm dead. I'm all in for it.

You may still be struggling to believe this for your *own* story. That's fine. You can borrow my belief until you've got enough of your own.

So, anchor in right here, in the truth of "your story matters." I'll hold the rope while you courageously venture into the world with your words.

Now that we have this foundation, join me in the following chapters as we dig into the strategies for moving through and beyond obstacles with ease.

"Give yourself permission to write a bad book. Writer's block is another name for writer's dread—the paralyzing fear that our work won't measure up. It doesn't matter how many books I've published, starting the next one always feels as daunting as the first. A day comes when I just have to make a deal with myself: write something anyway, even if it's awful. Nobody has to know. Maybe it never leaves this room! Just go."

—Barbara Kingsolver

CHAPTER TWO

what causes writer's block?

Now that we know your story matters, we need to get it into the world. In order to do that, we have to address the elephant in the room: the dreaded writer's block.

But what is it? Let's talk about what writer's block is and what it isn't.

We can't address it if we can't define it.

What do you think of when you think of writer's block?

Do you think of the person staring at a blank screen, uninspired and stuck on what to type next?

Really, writer's block is just one branch of what we also call *creative block*.

It's anytime a person is trying to do something creative, generally something they were *made* to do, feel good doing, and love... when suddenly they just *can't*.

It's been described by some as having as blank a mind as the screen or canvas or score they're staring at. There's just... nothing there. It's "a barrier to inspiration, an inability to access one's internal creativity."[1]

We've come to know (and fear) writer's block, then, as an inability to access our internal creativity around putting words on a page.

Here's what writer's block *isn't:*

An excuse.

It's also not permanent.

Nor is it a sign that you are or aren't a qualified writer.

In fact, creative blocks are part of the journey, so if you've experienced one—congratulations, you're a creative!

And if you haven't—yay! You probably will! But if not, double yay! You're a unicorn.

After years of coaching and writing, I've come to understand that we hold many myths about writer's block. In fact, I decided writer's block itself was a myth for a whole minute.

But this is where I've landed. Blocks are real. Therefore, writer's block is real.

What the block *is* and why it's there is full of myths and misperceptions.

You're welcome to my understanding or to formulate your own, but the gist is... there's absolutely no reason to stay stuck. None.

Forward movement is not only possible, but it's crucial.

In fact, writer's block is less your enemy and more your cautious friend tapping you on the shoulder and saying, "Hey, can you look at this for a sec?"

Most people miss the whisper and leap straight to panic. Many of us are hoping to pay our bills with our creative output! We don't have time to be blocked!

But the longer we chase down the wrong solution, the longer we stay stuck—the fewer bills we pay, the fewer people we impact, and the less legacy we leave behind.

So, here's my humble proposition: most people experience blocks, and most people misunderstand the purpose, meaning, and message of said blocks.

Creative blocks are a love letter to us, not our enemy. They are a message that something needs attention. They are the engine light in your car, irritating because you can see a bill in your near future, but so important because honoring that light keeps you from being stranded on the side of the road with an even bigger bill.

Over the years I've noticed some common themes of blocks, so that's what we're going to talk about from here on out.

These are the five most common forms of writer's block that I see from the hundreds of authors I've coached:

1. *Mental block*—our beliefs and thoughts can work against our creativity.
2. *Emotional block*—our fears, traumatic histories, and emotional responses will take us down in a flash.
3. *Scarcity block*—our sense of lack related to our resources of time, money, and know-how, as well as our creative energy and self-awareness, can prevent us from feeling equipped or motivated to move forward, blocking our work.
4. *Attentional block*—our focus and attention can easily be drawn away from our creativity due to personal life challenges, mental capacity, and neurology.
5. *Procedural block*—habits, routines, and workflow can be practical obstacles to creativity.

Not all creative blocks are created equal, therefore, they have different solutions to address them. Most of us will lean toward one or two; I imagine all of us will experience one of these types of blocks at some point or another. Much of who you are as an individual, your unique wiring and life experiences, will determine which of these you hang out in the most.

You'll also notice some overlap. The beliefs that hold us up (mental block) often come with an emotional response (emotional block). If we can address one, we can address both. Sometimes when we resolve the procedural block we find an emotional block lurking beneath the surface, cleverly using the procedural block as a mask. Don't let this distress you! This is basically all of life. You're not alone. You can hop around the next five sections however it best supports you to do so. With this reading, you may resonate most with attentional or scarcity blocks. Next time around, it might be mental blocks. This book is meant to be a coach in your corner every day, encouraging you right where *you* are.

To help you easily find the pro tips, I've included a section at the back called, "Pro Tips: Quick Reference Guide" where I've compiled the tips from each chapter for quick and easy access.

So, let's hop in already!

mental blocks

"Don't let mental blocks control you. Set yourself free. Confront your fear and turn the mental blocks into building blocks."

–Dr. Roopleen

CHAPTER THREE

mental blocks

THE GEEK OUT

WHAT ARE MENTAL BLOCKS? How do they prevent us from moving forward? I purposefully chose to start with mental blocks because they have the power to feed into every other block, hide *behind* every other block, getting totally missed in the hunt for solutions.

A mental block is "your brain reaching a barrier in accessing creativity, motivation, or productivity."[1] It's foggy brain or trouble processing information. Many of us experience mental blocks as an internal obstacle or resistance to accessing our creativity.

Taken a step further, mental blocks can be thoughts and beliefs getting in the way of our ability to perform a specific mental action. I say "can be" because mental blocks can also be the result of other issues, like a lack of sleep, nutrient deficiencies, and trauma, some of which we'll address in later chapters. For those, the solution is clear cut: sleep more, eat better, and address any medical reasons for the mental block. For non-medical reasons, let's consider the way our thoughts and beliefs impact our mental wellness and ability to think and process clearly as we're trying to write our books (this can also address trauma resistance, which I cover in depth in the next chapter).

Now, let's take a minute to geek out on our wonderful, beautiful brains, shall we?

THE GEEK OUT

Our minds matter. They are powerful, a bit mysterious, and totally underrated. We have a level of awareness that our thoughts and beliefs impact us, yet we live every day underutilizing the importance of this reality. We often live by default.

Your brain loves living by default.

Autopilot is one of its favorite functions. This isn't because your brain is lazy, just the opposite! It's because your brain is strategic—it has *a lot* to manage. So much so that it's delegated various tasks to different regions of the brain in order to focus, calling on the specialties of that region as needed. *As needed.* Because your brain has a budget of energy and needs to spend it well.

The more your brain can reserve energy, the more it can divert it to the places you need it most at any given moment. Thus, autopilot! For example, for most of us, the brain has nailed breathing. It doesn't take a lot of energy or any thought for you to breathe in and breathe out. In fact, you've been doing it this whole time. The fact that your brain can put that function on autopilot means you have some extra energy to divert to learning how to write and publish your book, overcoming every obstacle along the way.

When breathing suddenly needs attention, say in the case of an illness or injury, your brain must divert the extra energy it was spending elsewhere *back* to this crucial life-giving system to keep you alive. This can definitely lead to a mental block!

Because that's the other thing—your brain is focused on survival. In fact, that's the main reason it loves autopilot... it wants to prepare for worst-case scenarios, keeping a reserve of energy available for emergencies. Unfortunately, many of us override our brain and tax it until it's empty and exhausted. Cue burnout and creative blocks.

We can overtax our brain by not giving it enough processing time. One study shows that "scientists have measured the amount of data that enter the brain and found that an average person living today processes as much as 74 GB in information a day (that is as much as watching sixteen movies), through TV, computers, cell phones, tablets, billboards, and many other gadgets. Every year it is about five percent more than the previous year.[2] Only five hundred years ago, 74 GB of information would be what a highly educated person consumed in a lifetime, through books and stories."[3]

Since our brain is processing such large amounts of information, it must quickly decide what gets filed where—what gets immediate attention, what gets filed under "later," and what gets tossed to the rubbish bin immediately. It's doing all of this through the lens of its perception of your emotional and physical survival. All the time.

It's no wonder that sometimes we experience mental blocks in our creativity. Our minds are *busy*. But we have an opportunity and obligation to *help*. That's right, you can help your brain.

Help a Brain Out, Will Ya?

You've probably heard it said:

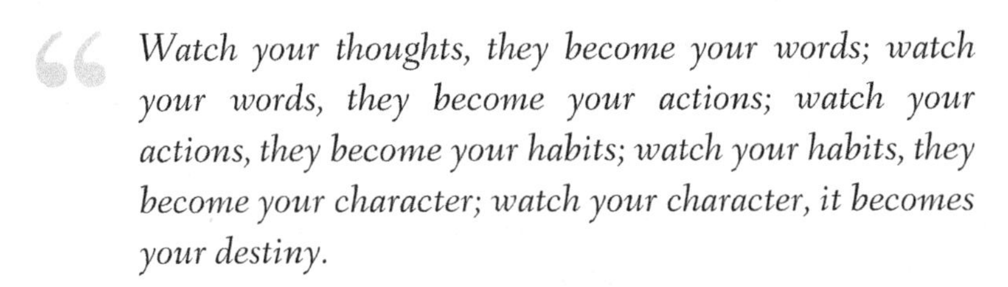

> *Watch your thoughts, they become your words; watch your words, they become your actions; watch your actions, they become your habits; watch your habits, they become your character; watch your character, it becomes your destiny.*
>
> *—Lao Tau*

Our thoughts are the source of everything that follows. If we don't pay attention *here*, we will end up in all sorts of trouble.

Our thoughts, untended, become beliefs. Beliefs sometimes drive us beyond our own rational reasoning. While we have some conscious awareness of the beliefs we hold, most of them are the iceberg beneath the surface. We don't realize they're there until our ship runs up against them.

Here's an example. The other day I was cooking breakfast. I *love* eggs in nearly any form. I was so relieved when "science" changed its mind and decided eggs weren't so high in cholesterol after all and we should eat more of them. Yes, please.

The other day I was pretty hungry. I really wanted *three* eggs. Yep, you read that right, three. As I debated grabbing the third egg, I noticed a sense of shame in me. I pulled the thread on the "shame" and found a thought at the other end. *If I eat three eggs, I'm being indulgent and gluttonous.* What?! I followed the thread a little further and it led me to the belief that had developed: *Only fat, ugly, unlovable, undisciplined people eat three eggs.* If *I* eat a third egg, I will have no excuse for the extra weight I carry around. Genetics, trauma, and hormones would all be dismissed as correlating causes of "extra weight," and the *third egg* would take the blame.

This is a true story.

I've lived by default with this story for *years*. I'm not entirely sure of its origin, but I can guess it came from the years when I worked hard to eat as few calories and fat as possible. It was a good day when all of my meals were made with fat-free, calorie-free synthetic non-foods. Somewhere in there, I'm sure the extra eighty calories of an additional egg took root as *the thing* to watch out for.

A friend joked the other day when I shared the story. "So you could have two eggs and a donut, but not three eggs?" Yep. Basically.

See how irrational? And yet So. Many. Years. of my life had been lived under the passive acceptance of this ridiculous notion. How many years had I successfully resisted the third egg for this reason? How many years had I snuck a third egg in, only to look in the mirror, *sure* that I'd fallen off the wagon and was back on the road to undesirable?

See how simple a thought can be? Yet the places it takes us are deep.

So, here's how you can help your brain.

We need to *direct* our thoughts, not *react* to them. This is where living by default doesn't always actually serve us. Collins Dictionary defines "by default" like this: "it happens only because something else which might have prevented it or changed it has not happened." This means that thoughts come and go, and you do nothing but passively integrate them. Reacting means leaving it to your brain, which is busy with surviving, to notice how you react and then make a decision on how to file that thought. This is handing all of your power over to a chemical system meant to survive, not thrive. So, take back the reins and help a brain out, will ya?

[illegible] And [illegible] Mama [illegible] [illegible] the [illegible] How many years had I successively relaxed the third egg [illegible] [illegible] only to look in the mirror [illegible] on the wall and was back [illegible] still fine?

So [illegible] simply [illegible]

Which is what can help your brain

We need to [illegible] [illegible] by default the [illegible] actually were [illegible] [illegible] [illegible] happens only because [illegible] [illegible] might have [illegible] [illegible] [illegible] [illegible] [illegible] [illegible] [illegible] [illegible] [illegible] with [illegible] [illegible] [illegible] [illegible] [illegible] to [illegible] [illegible] [illegible] [illegible] [illegible] back the [illegible] and [illegible] you.

CHAPTER FOUR

mental blocks

THE CHECK ENGINE LIGHT

ENGINE CHECK

In order to move from reacting to directing, we have to look for our engine light to indicate that we're headed for trouble.

You are most likely to notice the impact of your thoughts before you begin to recognize your thoughts while thinking them. That's okay! This is a process of slowing down and bringing mindfulness to our thought life. Many of us are so used to fast-paced info-overload processing *or* avoiding the silence of our minds, that we don't stop to listen to ourselves *at all*.

In this case, we need to reverse engineer our thought process, picking up responsibility for ourselves the moment we notice something is off.

Here are some warnings your "check engine light" might give you before you're aware of the thoughts taking you there.

- You're not making progress *at all*. Like, you're not even sitting down to open your notebook or digital file.

- You might feel too tired to do anything, let alone think or write productively.
- You might have trouble completing a train of thought...
- You might feel like all of your mental processes have slowed waaaaaaay down. Your reaction time is slower. Processing the words people are saying to you is delayed. You have to read and re-read and re-read the same line to understand what it's saying.
- You might keep procrastinating (ahem, avoiding) working on your book. This will look like a *decision* to work on your book, but something else taking precedence last second (even if it's finally turning the house upside down to find all the missing pairs of socks in the pile in your closet).
- Similar to procrastinating, you might find yourself easily distracted. Every ding from your phone wins your attention or a random thought that enters your head gets some form of action. For me, this might be a sudden urge to clean my garage, check my texts, or clean the litter box. When my good friend has a project to start (or complete), he'll clear his email inbox, clean his bathroom, or suddenly need to water his flowers.
- You might feel *nothing*. As in, you may find yourself staring off into space, with no real thoughts to capture, just... staring.

This isn't an exhaustive list, but if you're experiencing a mental block, you'll see yourself on it somewhere.

Remember, that list is the error code for the check engine light. We need to get beneath the hood to see what's *really* going on.

CHAPTER FIVE

mental blocks

BENEATH THE HOOD

BENEATH THE HOOD

A 2020 STUDY found that we have, on average, six thousand thoughts per day.[1] That's a LOT of thinking! Those thoughts flow in... then what? Well, if we're living by default, those thoughts can recklessly become beliefs; become actions; become destiny. Do you want just *any* thought to become your destiny? No! So, we need to be willing to chase them down as soon as we're able.

This is a practice in metacognition, the process of thinking about one's own thinking. It's hard! But so important.

Let's look beneath the hood at some of the "check engine" error codes.

The mental block behaviors we can *see* are exhaustion and fatigue, lack of motivation and progress, easily distracted ("Squirrel!"), feeling numb, a slower reaction time, etc.

But what's *really* going on?

If mental blocks are often the result of thoughts and beliefs, then what are those thoughts and beliefs? I'm so glad you asked.

Today I sat in a café to work on this chapter. I needed to get away from the distractions of home. I nested myself in the corner with the cozy chairs, threw on my noise-canceling headphones, and downed my peach smoothie while I geeked out on the brain and *you*.

A few hours in I found myself staring off into space. The writing had become challenging. My outline wasn't as strong or helpful as I wanted. I felt rambly (I trust I've fixed that for you by now) and aimless. So, instead of writing, I was staring (yep, my "check engine light" was on). Suddenly, my metacognition kicked in and I became aware of my own thinking. *You're literally the worst writer ever. Who do you think you are writing this book? Just quit already. You were an eighteen-hit wonder, and this is nineteen. Stick to publishing* other *people's books.* *Ouch*

Fortunately, I was writing a book on writer's block and couldn't give in. Who would I be if the author of the life-changing book for writers to push through stagnation *got derailed by writer's block?!* (Spoiler Alert: I still sometimes do. *Eek*) No!

So, I took that thought, ugly as it was, and I held it up to the light. I quickly studied it, decided it was trash, and tossed it aside. I would not be deterred... this time. Because I know the truth, having had to repeat it *so* many times to myself and to my clients.

1. No first draft is good. They're all fairly awful. That's how they're supposed to be. They aren't the version we publish. Plus, I can work with any words... I can't work with a blank page. Therefore, I'm *not* the worst writer ever, but I *am* writing a "Stormy First Draft" or SFD (as Brené Brown calls it in her book, *Rising Strong*) and it's going to feel kinda crappy at times.

2. Who do I think I am? Just a writer trying to help other writers. If I write even *one* "aha" that moves you forward to the next step, then it's worth it. I mean it. That's who I am.
3. While quitting is definitely always an option, I value keeping my word to myself and to the people I've promised this book. There's no quitting. This thought allowed me to recommit to myself that I'm *doing this.*

When we don't catch our thoughts, they become our beliefs. We tell ourselves stories over and over until we believe them.

Here are some stories I'm sure you're familiar with.

"I don't belong here."

This one pops up a lot. Ever been to a conference with other writers, some really famous, some just a little more famous than you, and said, "I don't belong here"?

Welcome to Imposter Syndrome.

I know the Imposter Syndrome is over-talked about, but that's because it's real.

It's a deep belief that you're not good enough for the task in front of you, that somehow, you've faked it this far and are about to be exposed for the fraud you are at any second. If we dig even deeper, it's a threat that if you're discovered, your greatest fear will be the truth staring you in the face: you're a nobody. You have no significance. You have nothing of value to offer, therefore you are nothing.

Makes doing the dishes pretty exciting, right? If we have the choice to risk the exposure of our very worth and value or clean days-old crap off the cutlery, we'll call it writer's block and scrape the scum. That's without self-awareness. With it, we can call it what it is (a lie) and get our stories out there.

The truth is, your story matters and no one is more qualified to tell it than you are. Your life has worth and the power to impact others. Believing anything less keeps your light from the dark world.

Pro Tip: Ever been impacted by someone else's story? They felt like an imposter too. What if they'd kept their light to themselves? Remember that and put words on that page. You're the only one who can.

"I'm not good enough."

Welcome to the world of perfectionism, where we elevate the idea that "good enough" is achievable and whoever is holding the measuring stick is sure to give us a trophy when we finally arrive.

It's not measurable and no one actually knows who's measuring anyway. It seems to be a standard we each internalize for ourselves, ensuring that we never quite achieve "enough." (This is partly why I wrote my children's book, *Tercules.* It's about being "just right" the way you are... we all need that message!)

If we get even deeper beneath the hood with perfectionism, we often find a belief that our worth is somehow attached to our achievements (and failures). If I don't succeed, then I fail, and if I fail, I confront my fear as truth: I'm a loser. Yet all of this is a story we make up! When we live from a belief that our worth and value are found in what we can *do*, we will exhaust ourselves trying to please unappeasable people—namely, ourselves. Our survival brain will kick in to keep us from our perception of total annihilation, making writing a book pretty dang hard.

Here's the truth: your worth and value have nothing to do with your achievements. I know that's hard to believe if this is your mental block, so I'll say it again, but louder. YOUR WORTH AND VALUE HAVE NOTHING TO DO WITH YOUR ACHIEVEMENTS.

It doesn't matter if your parents told you so, your church told you so, your partner told you so, your best friend told you so, or the childhood bully told you so. They're all *wrong*.

You are valuable and worthy of every love and affection just for being *you*. Say it out loud: "I am valuable and worthy of every love and affection just for being me." That's right.

Even if your book flops, you still published a book, something eighty percent of the population wants to do, but only about three percent succeed at. (Also, books tend to flop due to poor marketing, not poor writing. Some poorly written but well-marketed books do well. I'm just saying, it's a faulty association in every way possible).

Now that your entire existence isn't attached to what you do, can you give yourself permission to be human? To be on a journey? To write a stormy first draft? Remember, *every published author* with a *great* book had a team to get them there: editors, beta readers, cover designers, interior designers, formatters, and on and on. Don't compare your stormy first draft to The New York Times Best Seller in the airport bookstore. You have *no idea* what that book's stormy draft looked like (and I bet it was worse than yours).

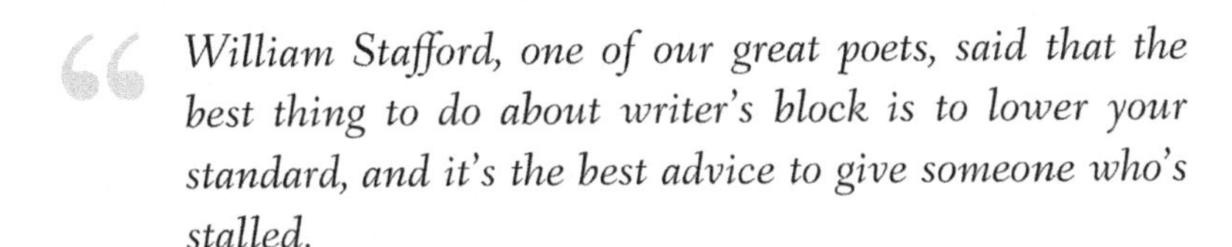

> *William Stafford, one of our great poets, said that the best thing to do about writer's block is to lower your standard, and it's the best advice to give someone who's stalled.*
>
> *—Ted Kooser*
>
> *I haven't had writer's block. I think it's because my process involves writing very badly.*
>
> *—Jennifer Egan*

Pro Tip: The best way to overcome perfectionism is to practice imperfection. Yep. Let yourself start writing. Write anything! And let it be trash. The great thing about writing is you can burn the paper or delete the page. So let yourself be stormy as all get out just to let your body experience it. You might be surprised by what comes from it!

"Everything is against me."

I won't lie and say I've never thought this. There have definitely been days when I've been fairly convinced I was simply placed on earth to make others feel better about their own lives.

It's just not true. And it certainly doesn't serve you to believe it.

Our Reticular Activating System, RAS, is a bundle of nerves that live in your brainstem. One of its jobs is to determine what information gets processed and what doesn't. However, the brainstem is the seat of your subconscious, meaning that your RAS is engaging what lives *there*.

> The Reticular Activating System just reinforces what's in your subconscious. So, if your thought (belief) in a neural pathway is "I don't like exercise," guess what: You'll battle to get into a fitness routine. Because your RAS will only filter information that will make you avoid exercise at all costs. To the point where it will block information about any fitness successes you might achieve.
>
> And that's one of the most NB things to know about your neural pathways and RAS: It's an automatic process that cannot distinguish between good and bad behavior. Your RAS does not care whether getting fit is good or bad for you. It only automates what's in your neural pathways (LifeXchange).[2]

Basically, when you allow thoughts to enter your mind passively, those thoughts create neural pathways that tell your RAS to look for signs to prove that thought true. Simplified, it's like this: If you think, "I'd love to move to Alaska. It's a beautiful place and I'd be happy there," your RAS will begin to highlight any information it finds related to Alaska. You'll be *sure* it's a sign you're supposed to move there! In reality, you told your RAS, by allowing thoughts to pass unfiltered, to begin bringing anything Alaska-related to your conscious.

Therefore, if you allow the thought, "Everything is against me," to enter without challenge, your RAS will begin to shine a light on every piece of evidence that you're *right*, purposefully dismissing all evidence *against* that thought.

As I said, your brain is powerful! And without some stewardship, it can take you down some difficult paths.

One more thing about pessimism—if we dig a little deeper, we find a fear of disappointment. It feels easier to prepare ourselves for disappointment than to expect something good... that goes south. The problem with this faulty thinking is that you're *still* disappointed when your pessimism proves "true." It's choosing to live in a space of disappointment in order to avoid disappointment. It's self-defeating and yet one of the biggest "strategies" so many people take with life and their expectations. This is where the RAS further reinforces our pessimism, which we taught it to do.

Pro Tip: Be intentional about the thoughts you think. Grab them when you can and make sure they are serving you. I use an app called "I Am." It gives me regular notifications with "I am" statements (that I can customize to serve the thoughts I'm trying to re-work). It gives me messages I can use to replace faulty beliefs I've developed (sometimes thinking of a positive thought after living with a negative one for so long is challenging). Do *something* to give your RAS a new thought or belief to reinforce, starting with, "It's not that everything is against me... it's that life is sometimes challenging and doesn't always go my way. I choose to believe that the new path will be even better than the one I thought I wanted. I can't wait to see how this will be used for my good!"

"I need to know the whole process before I can start."

Some people actually *do* need to see the whole process before they can start. It's part of their wiring to want details and a plan. These people, however, diligently get that information as soon as possible so they can keep their momentum.

Other people, however, use a thought like this to stall their progress. It's a form of control that sabotages their ability to keep moving forward. "Well, I guess I don't have ALL of the information that could be had on this topic, sooooooo..."

Here's the blockbuster: you don't actually need to know the whole process before you start. In fact, some of you really *shouldn't* know the whole process before you start because it will overwhelm you into paralysis.

All you need to know is *the next step*.

Take one step at a time and you *will* finish writing your book and you will get it published. This is true for your writing process as well. "I don't know the whole plot line yet, soooooo..." Keep writing anyway! You may not know the whole plot, but I bet you can knock out the next scene. Or the next paragraph. Or the next line. There's a whole wonderful group of people called Pantsers who write by the "seat of their pants," so yes, it can be (and is) done.

If we dig deeper beneath the hood, we find that the drive to be in control can be a response to deep anxiety. The control, then, presents as a coping strategy and an attempt toward safety. This is an opportunity to tell yourself a new story. "I don't need to know the whole process to keep working toward my goal. I trust myself to find exactly what I need to take the next step. That next step is progress toward my goal of impacting other lives for good with my book. I will know what I need to know just in time to act on it." Moving from a place of fear and helplessness to a place of assurance and a plan ("I'll learn what I need before the next step.") dislodges the mental block and sets you on a path forward.

Pro Tip: If you find yourself thinking that you can't move forward until you have more information, try one of these:

1. Do the *very next thing* that you *can* do.

2. Ask someone who knows what you need to know. Sometimes asking for guidance *is* the next step, so take it. There are wonderful communities out there set up for *just this purpose*, like my illustrator and writer community, *The Writer's Block*. See a theme? We offer community support, expert interviews, and group coaching calls so that each person *always has access* to knowing their next step.

3. Pause, set a timer for fifteen or thirty minutes, research your heart out, then get back to writing.

4. If you're writing fiction, try asking your character! On a number of occasions, I've encouraged authors to do a character interview with the characters in the scene or plot point they are stuck on. There are a variety of character interview questions you can google and use, or create your own. The important thing is that as you ask questions, you write the first thing that comes to mind, no matter how strange. Yes, I'm asking you to let your fictional character speak to you!

5. Sometimes it helps to role-play the character interview. My daughter was recently stuck on a plot point in her story. I played the role of interviewer and asked her to answer as her character. She was

desperate to get unstuck and was willing to let me be a little "weird" about getting the answers she needed. As I asked her character questions, I had my daughter answer out loud the first thoughts that came to mind. Her plot revealed itself right in front of us. "WHY does that WORK?" she asked. Who knows? But when it does, it's pure magic.

"I don't matter."

One of my clients said this the other day, and it simultaneously resonated and broke my heart. This thought is really a deep core question, "Do I matter?" It may *feel* like a statement, but it's nearly always a question. This question often leads us to exhaustion, trying to prove that we *do* matter. In the case of my client, she constantly sacrificed her own dreams and goals for *anything* anyone around her needed. In order to matter, she had to stop mattering to herself. This is tragic and yet so pervasive in our society.

Before I can go any further, I have to stop and say: YOU DO MATTER. You do. You don't have to earn it. And most likely the people you're trying to prove it to can't adequately demonstrate the great worth you hold. No human can.

The strange irony of this statement is that it quickly becomes a verb. *Mattering* becomes action. When you believe you matter, you act like it. You will treat yourself like someone deserving of time, attention, affection, and kindness, just like you do for so many other people. If you don't treat yourself like you matter, many other people won't either. This is lame but true. You must treat yourself with the same dignity and kindness that you give to the other people you esteem.

One of the ways to do that is to prioritize your own dreams and goals. It's not mean or selfish or ungodly to believe you have a calling and purpose and value on this earth and to choose to honor that.

This is all too common among parents, mothers especially. I remember believing that my kids should be *everything*. My whole world pre-children was supposed to halt and I was supposed to revolve around the little developing humans in order to be a "good mom." Don't get me wrong, children cause our lives to pivot and our attention to shift. They should! But many of us have been taught to take it too far, to the detriment of our children.

I remember sitting in a writing conference when this topic came up. The speaker said, "Do you want to teach your children that when *they* grow up and become moms and dads, they're not allowed to have dreams anymore? That they aren't allowed to pursue their life calling between the ages of zero to eighteen of their children?"

This was such an epiphany for me. No! I want my kids to know that their lives matter no matter what stage they're in. That they get to pursue their purpose and calling regardless of taking on the "parent" role.

Kids catch what we model, not what we teach. So, show them what it looks like to be a healthy, multi-dimensional human who can both deeply love and nurture their children as well as pursue hobbies or vocations they've been called to. Not to mention that it's so psychologically confusing for children to experience being the literal center of their parents' universe. We've called that "good" in our culture for too long, to the detriment of the mental health of our children *and* their parents. It does not prepare our children for real life outside the home, where they will *not* be the center of the universe.

Don't hear what I'm not saying. I'm not saying that you should pursue your every desire *at the expense* of your relationship with your kids. But I *am* saying that it's okay to show them what a life that matters looks like... yours, then theirs. You get to show them that it's okay to get away for a weekend for a writing retreat. They'll survive. You get to show them that Mommy has dreams and goals and this is what it looks like to pursue them! They'll have a roadmap of their own. You get to show them that Daddy overcomes challenges because he believes in helping others with his story, because his story matters. You're giving your children permission to let their stories matter too.

Pro Tip: When you notice that thought come into your awareness, intentionally do something to show yourself that you *do* matter. Take time to love the little child inside of you who still needs a hug, reassurance, and a reminder that they're seen, heard, and valued. Don't wait until you hear the message... show yourself kindness anyway. Remember, giving yourself a positive belief like "I matter" will train your RAS to reinforce it with the life around you. As you take the first steps toward believing your life and story matter, you'll begin to see evidence of it everywhere. But you have to take the first step. Do something kind for yourself today that you'd only do for someone you really love and value.

"This is taking too long and I'm falling behind."

I hear this all. the. time. "I'm behind!" It's so easy to set up an expectation for ourselves about how long this process of writing and publishing should take. This is especially true if you joined a course or program and feel that everyone in your cohort is moving faster than you are. They might be! But that doesn't mean you're behind. This becomes a source of panic and anxiety, which only moves you from the cognitive part of your brain (where you put meaning to words) to the fight-or-flight part of your brain, which gets hyper-focused on surviving and safety, thus avoiding the very thing causing you discomfort. This is why many of us do *less* when we feel we're behind, only increasing overwhelm and the sense of "being behind." It's a loop that can be hard to get out of.

A few things are happening when we think we're falling behind.

1. This is an indicator that you have established expectations for yourself.

2. These expectations appear to either be out of line with what's realistic for you *or* there's a block that needs unblocking so you can hop back in.

3. Now that you've begun, you realize that there's way more to this writing-a-book thing than you realized. The "cost" is higher than you expected. This leads to *impatience.*

According to *Psychology Today,* "Impatience is triggered when we have a goal, and realize it's going to cost us more than we thought to reach it."[3] It's the result of perceiving that things aren't going our way and we think they really should.

I caught this in myself recently. I invested in a program to help me scale up my business so I'm freed up to help more people. The investment was significant and it's a 90-day program. In this case, falling behind means *to me* that I have a very limited amount of time to access the support I need in order to grow. I've also assigned a meaning: if I *don't* access the support that I hired to help me, then I've wasted my money and I'm probably life's biggest failure.

See how quickly we can make up stories? That level of pressure can cause anxiety, which is not the healthiest part of the brain for good decision-making! I heard myself say, "I've gotten behind," and realized those were empty words that I could actually give depth to! I contacted my coach and asked for deadlines. And guess what, within an hour I had my next deadline. And it was in the future, which meant I wasn't behind after all. As soon as I asked for help and got guidance, all the anxiety around "I'm behind" fell away and I was able to make progress on my coursework.

Pro Tip: When you hear yourself thinking that you're behind, pause and dig deeper. How do you know you're "behind?" Who says? If you're in a program like the one I'm in (with a time limit), then make a plan to pace yourself and get back on track. You may find you need deadlines, like me, accountability, a strategic plan, or discipline (all of which I cover in upcoming chapters). OR you may find that the expectation is self-imposed and can be adjusted. Sometimes we think we can do more than we can with our busy lives... so adjust as you need to. Just *keep moving forward.*

If you're simply trying to hit a writing or publishing goal, then either make a plan to hit your goal, or adjust your goal. It's really okay to publish your book a week or a month later than you thought. If that causes any anxiety in you, then pause and ask why.

CHAPTER SIX

mental blocks

GRAB THE WRENCH

GRAB THE WRENCH

THE PRO TIPS throughout the chapters give you practical tips for overcoming that form of mental block *today*. Try them out and see which one moves you forward, even at all.

The main thing to remember is that if you notice the signs of mental blocks when your "check engine" light comes on, stop the car! Get beneath the hood and see what's going on. What thoughts are sneaking up on you, reinforcing false beliefs? Take notice of any feelings in your body and ask yourself questions about them. Why did this shame rise up when I wanted a third egg for breakfast? Why is my head foggy? What's that tightness in my chest? Flip the switch on your metacognition, like tuning into a radio station, and listen to your thoughts.

Once you notice a thought or feeling, chase it down. Go deeper. Is it true you're a loser for thinking you can write a book? If so, why? And what does being a loser mean to you? What's the worst thing that can happen to a published loser? Who defines "loser" anyway? Are they credible? Why do they get to determine your fate? Bring your curiosity and challenge any of the questions or beliefs that have you derailed. Tell yourself the truth, a better story, and get back on the road!

CHAPTER SEVEN

mental blocks

BACK ON THE ROAD

GET BACK ON THE ROAD

I USED to walk around believing a story I told myself about worthlessness. From a young age, I picked up some false beliefs that I was unlovable, unattractive, undesirable, and all-around worthless. The world can be a hard place to live in, and often these false beliefs were reinforced by my external environment. So much so, that my RAS kicked in, and even if something *tried* to show me my true value, I couldn't see it. All I could see was the overwhelming amount of evidence that I was indeed worthless.

The sense of smallness and worthlessness was exploited by people who used it to control and manipulate me. And I let them because I thought I deserved it. With that, I picked up a *new* false belief: I'm not worth fighting for.

Whether friendship or life partner, every experience with abandonment solidified the message that I wasn't worth fighting for *at all.* (I was once even verbally told I wasn't worth fighting for.)

One day, my metacognition kicked in and I *heard* the thought. *I'm not worth fighting for.* With that thought came the deepest levels of grief and sadness. It was powerful. It was disturbing. I still remember exactly where I was when I heard it. It had been there all along, but this time I *heard* it.

I decided to try out a new story. I pulled it out like a luxury dress from a high-end retailer. It said, "I'm absolutely worth fighting for (and I am) but some people aren't capable (or willing) of fighting for very worthy people like me. How sad for them; they lose so much."

It fit surprisingly well. And it was free. The new story swept over me and immediately cleaned house. It literally kicked "I'm not worth fighting for" to the curb, and then set up a victory parade to let everyone else know that *they're* worth fighting for too... it's just that some people aren't in for the fight. The Bible says that we shouldn't cast our pearls to swine, lest they trample them and tear us to pieces (Matthew 7:6), so I stopped.

Counteract the false thought with a true thought. Tell yourself a new story. Your perceptions are not an accurate reflection of your ability to knock this book out of the park or not... that's up to you.

Remember why your book matters to you. Is it worth the risk? (The answer is yes). If you're not sure, ask a friend. Or maybe ask a good friend anyway.

Then get back on the road!

In the next chapter, we're going to talk about *emotional blocks*. While both emotional and mental blocks happen primarily internally, there are some distinctions we're going to walk through together. Now that we understand mental blocks, we're ready to attack their emotional responses.

You can't think yourself out of a writing block; you have to write yourself out of a thinking block.

—John Rogers

emotional blocks

"I think writer's block is a bad name for a number of real problems facing writers, most notably of which is fear. Typically, when I feel blocked, I'm really afraid...What do I do when I feel blocked? I write through the block...I push through the discomfort, so that I can keep going. Momentum is a writer's friend."

—Jeff Goins

CHAPTER EIGHT

emotional blocks

THE GEEK OUT

You sit down to put words to the page. You blink. Tap your fingers. Scroll TikTok or Instagram.

Or both. You pray. Beg. Cry. Pee. And then, quit.

"I hate writer's block," you say as you grab the remote and click.

Many important stories *never get shared.*

Why? Because of what has become known as "writer's block," or what I like to call, "The Big Excuse to Enable Your Fear, Insecurity, and Laziness."

That's right, the BEEYFIL.

Don't get me wrong, the blank screen (and blank mind) are real! Writer's block becomes the perfect excuse for keeping it blank. I mean, what can you do to change it? #Netflix

Well, that's what you used to think. Now you know that multiple reasons for blocks keep us from achieving our goals and dreams.

One of those blocks is tricksy. Emotional blocks. Yep, those sneaky blocks show up like pretty little river pebbles but trip us up like the boulders they are.

Picture this: You decide, "Today's the day I'm going to start my book!" You watch the clock with anticipation, so excited to knock this goal out of the park and prove all the naysayers wrong. You know, the people who told you how hard it was to write and publish a book, and that maybe you could just serve at the local food distribution instead. You'll show them!

The clock strikes one and you're headed to get your booty in the seat. About halfway to your writing space, you take a big yawn. Your head clouds over. Man, you sure are tired. And hungry. And maybe a little hangry. You pause in the kitchen to grab a snack, fill up your water (gotta stay hydrated for all that goal-chasing you're about to do) and knock back a Tylenol, just in case. You turn to head to your seat when you notice that one solitary dish. You really should just clean it. Then you'll be able to focus better. Suddenly you've cleaned the whole house, done the laundry, and washed down the inside of the fridge.

It's not too late! You can still get started! You finally make it to your seat and... man, the surface is dusty. How'd you miss this surface? No problem, it's wiped down. You pull open your document, pull out your notes... when one of a few things happens. You might suddenly feel a lot of yucky feelings but can't place them. Or you might feel no feelings and realize you actually have nothing to say after all. You might feel your heart rate pick up a bit, your tummy churn a little, and the otherwise silent blank word document screaming at you to do something, anything, for your book. You get up and walk away.

What in the world just happened?! You were so excited to write this book! To impact your readers! To see your life experiences benefit others for good! You hate doing dishes!

This, my friend, is a classic case of an Emotional Block.

THE GEEK OUT

Hang with me a minute while I geek out on *why your brain* is trying to prevent you from telling your story.

Emotional blocks can show up as tiredness, a dirty sock that suddenly and desperately needs its pair, a sudden craving for tacos from that one and only place, or the call of your bed to come rest your eyes a little.

In reality, emotional blocks are made of up our fears, traumatic histories, and emotional responses. An emotional block is our brain's way of protecting us, once again, from a perception of a threat to our life (emotional and physical). Remember! Your fight-or-flight system is a response to perceived threats, *including your sense of belonging, identity, and emotional safety.*

When we sit in our memories, our brain doesn't venture with us into the past. It remains fully aware of you in the *present.* When memories surface, your brain and body experience those memories *in the present.* This is one thing that therapists like me are especially aware of when working with people with unprocessed trauma. If we lead them too quickly into those parts of their brain, the result can be re-traumatization... a re-injury in the present from the traumatizing memory.

Well, guess what? Your brain would like *anything* but to take you back to places of pain and injury. If your story is set to include any hard part of your own life experience, you can expect emotional blocks. This doesn't make you ill-equipped to write a book, incapable of telling your story, or not good enough to see your book published. Emotional blocks are your check engine light letting you know something needs attention! And that "something" is you... your heart, your mind, and your body. What a beautiful gift your brain wants to give you!

But if you don't know better, you'll think they're only pebbles but end up tripping on boulders. You'll keep self-sabotaging and avoiding the very thing you want to do... put your messy but important story into the world.

CHAPTER NINE

emotional blocks

THE CHECK ENGINE LIGHT

ENGINE CHECK

LET'S take a closer look at those pebbles, shall we?

On the surface, you won't recognize your traumas, life injuries, or deepest fears. Instead, you'll notice changes in some of your everyday, automatic functions.

You might notice that:

- You're not sleeping well, either unable to fall asleep, waking up too early, or not feeling rested after sufficient hours of sleep.
- Your eating patterns are off: you're slipping into past, less healthy eating patterns, not remembering to eat, or hyper-focusing on your next meal.
- You're taking shallow breaths and yawning more frequently.
- You're feeling feelings but not knowing what they are... you may respond with attempts to avoid or distract from the discomfort.

- You're not able to find the words to communicate what you're feeling.
- In extreme cases, you've begun to experience intense anxiety or panic attacks.
- You're unusually withdrawing from people and social situations.
- You're beginning to feel distant from your desire to write your story (dissociation).
- You're feeling completely paralyzed in decision-making, maybe even catching your eyes feeling wide open or clenching your jaw.
- You're finally doing all of the small, menial tasks that have been in the back of your mind forever, like reorganizing the storage boxes, pulling the weeds you've walked past for months, or making sure all of the colored pencils are nice and sharp the next time someone wants to use them.
- You're unusually short or cold in your responses to other humans, quick to lose your patience or temper, more defensive than usual, or more argumentative than normal.

This list isn't exhaustive, of course, and other correlating factors can come into play that should be considered. For example, some of these, like sleep and diet, can also be medical issues. Or maybe you're hosting a wedding reception in your yard and those darn weeds have finally got to go!

Unless you've got an exception, you're probably looking at some form of emotional block disguised as a pebble.

Let's get beneath the hood and see those pebbles for what they really are.

CHAPTER TEN

emotional blocks

BENEATH THE HOOD

BENEATH THE HOOD

When I said that emotional blocks are deceptive, rolling around like little pretty pebbles, I wasn't kidding. They're not just an irritation in our shoes (which, don't get me wrong... a pebble in the shoe of a giant can take him down), they're a toe-breaking boulder.

Before I over-villainize your emotional blocks, let me remind you that this is your brain *loving you*. It wants to protect you from the pain you might find if you sit and listen to your thoughts. The problem is that your brain is trying to make decisions *for you*. But you're capable of responding instead of reacting!

Let's take a look at what you've been reacting to so you can plan a response instead (i.e., overcome writer's block and get that cursor moving again!).

Fear of Failure

You're probably pretty familiar with the concept of fearing failure. Most of us have a very strong resistance to seeing ourselves as falling short of our dream or goal. We don't want *others* to witness our failure and think negatively of us and *we* don't want to live with the shame of our humanity—that we're not perfect. When we dig a little deeper beneath the hood, we find there are more stories we've told ourselves (or believed from others) about what it means to fail.

Some people have held stories that say failure means they are worthless and don't deserve love or respect or the right to exist. Whoa! If your brain holds a perception of failure as a threat to your very worth and right to exist, guess what? It's going to do everything in its power to *keep you alive.* Especially *not writing,* because why risk your very life?! See how important the stories that have taken root in our souls are? Our brain acts on them for our preservation.

But we can change the story!

What if, instead of failure meaning, "I'm worthless and don't deserve my place on the planet," I changed the story to something like Edison's on his journey to inventing the lightbulb? "When a reporter asked, 'How did it feel to fail one thousand times?' Edison replied, "I didn't fail one thousand times. The light bulb was an invention with one thousand steps.'"

Rather than a story defining his worth, Edison saw his not-getting-the-lightbulb-to-light attempts as steps of a process to success. Had he quit, we'd all still be sitting in the dark by candlelight (*or* someone else's name would hold the reputation of succeeding).

Edison is also quoted as saying: "I have not failed seven hundred times. I've succeeded in proving seven hundred ways how not to build a lightbulb."

He chose a story about failure that led his brain to a place of curiosity and growth versus the fight-or-flight many of us have trained our brains to associate it with. This enabled him to persevere, learn from his "mistakes," and overcome countless obstacles to his belief that a bulb could be filled with light.

Your brain wants to keep you alive. In a place of threat, it will do so by causing your system to fight (get agitated, moody, and short-tempered), run (avoid by doing *anything* else), or freeze (paralysis and numbness).

In a non-threatening situation, your brain wants to keep you alive by attaining new skills that you might eventually need to, you got it, stay alive. Your brain releases endorphins, dopamine, adrenaline, and other feel-good chemicals to drive your attention toward the stories it wants to learn from. Edison's brain appears to have held a story that light could be a great life-saving tool.

Edison *easily* could have chosen a route of despair and fear instead. But for whatever reason, he directed his thoughts to a place of growth and possibility, training his perception that mistakes and "failures" were *good,* necessary, and important for attaining his goal.

How about you? What if you took your fear of failure and trained it into a belief that expanded your vision rather than squelching it?

What if, when you sit down to type, you pay attention to the pebbles in your shoes and ask good questions? "Why am I so antsy right now? What's going on?" You might discover a fear that you'll publish your book, people will hate it and leave horrible reviews, and you'll have to move to the northernmost part of Alaska to hide in shame for the rest of your life. That fear might also tell you that people hating your book means your other fear was *true,* you were just kidding yourself thinking you could help people or write a decent book. If we follow that fear just a few inches more, we'll start to step into your feelings of worth. From antsy to worthless.

If you look close enough, that pebble will turn into a boulder... and if you give it a big hug, it will become a steppingstone.

How do you hug a boulder? You tell yourself the truth. It's like a pufferfish... it makes itself bigger to look scary and intimidating. But really, it's just a cute little fish trying to stay alive in a sea of actual giants.

While I don't recommend hugging a pufferfish, I *do* recommend hugging your boulder. Tell it that *every writer ever* wrote horrible first and second and third drafts. And that every horrible draft got better with revisions, and you're going to revise too. And then, every great book invited a team of editors and beta readers and publishers and cover designers and copywriters (and whoever else you might need) to make it the best possible version of itself. And also, every writer ever had *someone* who didn't love (maybe even hated) the book... and that's okay. That person is there to teach you who your book is for and who it isn't.

Hug your boulder with all the truth and love you can offer. Before you know it, it will light up as the next step on your path, and you won't be able to stop the words pouring from your soul.

Pro Tip: Ask yourself, "What's the story I've believed about failure? What do I think it's saying about me? What am I worried people will think about me? Why?" Keep digging deeper. If your answer is, "Failure says I'm a worthless loser," then ask yourself, "Why? Is it true?" Don't settle for a superficial answer. Remember, your engine light is just an indicator that something beneath the hood needs attention. Give it that attention! Don't let stories of failure become emotional blocks to getting your message into the world!

Fear of Success

Surprised? Yeah, I was too the first time I saw this boulder in someone's shoe. Since then, I've seen it countless times, always lurking just beneath the surface.

I remember sitting with a client one day and processing with her why she was feeling stuck. We talked about a possible fear of failure because so many people have that fear. But as we chatted, she began to process being afraid of losing control of her life if the book did well.

"Wait," I asked. "Are you afraid of succeeding?"

She thought for a second and said, "Yeah, actually, that's it. I *am* afraid of succeeding. What if I write this book and people love it? And it does really well? What if I'm suddenly overwhelmed with invitations to speak in places or do interviews or show up and sell the book? I love my life right now. I love my job right now; I don't want to give up my job." It was so interesting to hear her process those thoughts out loud. Honestly, it hadn't struck me before that moment that someone might be afraid of doing so well, of succeeding, that they might lose control of their own life.

I reminded her gently that she would always, always hold agency over her own life. Even if her book went on to become the best-selling book in the entire world for all time, she would still have a right to say no to anything she didn't want to participate in. She could say no to any interview, speaking engagement, or opportunity to show up. She could absolutely keep the job that she currently had and continue living the life that she loves.

Yes, there would probably be some adjustments to make. And she could make decisions one at a time as they came. But the important part was that she would continue to get to make her own decisions.

Here's the thing about fearing success. It's really a fear of losing control. Most of us are writing because we want to impact the world in some way. We want to change the lives of people that we care about, people who maybe were or are like us. They might be just a couple of steps behind where we've come from, and we want to help them along. Fear of success is not necessarily a fear of actually helping the people we want to help or seeing their lives changed in the ways that we want to see their lives changed. Fear of success is, then, also a fear of letting go. It's a fear of change, as my client highlighted. It's a fear of discomfort, the unknown, and the ways the unknown might surprise us negatively.

Fear of success can also be a fear of exposure. Some of us like our private little life. We've watched celebrities, our entire lives, lose their right to privacy, with paparazzi at every turn. We've watched them have to hide behind hats and sunglasses. We've joined the whole world in witnessing private, intimate moments as they were captured and blasted over the entire Internet. Yes, we want to change lives. But we don't want to lose ours in the process.

These are important messages to capture when we feel that flutter of stress in our chest as we're trying to finish our book and just can't get past the next sentence. You might be tempted to assume that yours is a fear of failure... but pause to consider: is it maybe a fear of success? What would it mean for you to succeed? What if your book went on and became the bestseller of all time? What fears do you feel rise up in you as you ask yourself that question?

Try journaling your thoughts to these questions:

"What would success look like for me?"

"What feelings do I notice when I picture that level of success?"

"Are those feelings positive? Negative? A mix of both?"

"What do I feel in my body when I imagine that success?"

"What fears do I notice when I imagine that level of success?"

"What are those fears telling me about myself?"

"What's *true*?" Start your sentence, 'Even if my book becomes the best-selling book of all time, I can/will/am...'

Pro Tip:

Your brain gets stuck when it feels helpless. If we are used to reacting instead of responding, then we will simply stay stuck and not understand why. If, however, you slow down and intentionally decide to *choose* your response, you can get yourself unstuck. So, when you are staring at a blank page (or can't even get your butt in the chair to look at the blank page), check your engine light... it's probably on. Get beneath the hood and ask yourself what's going on. Why are you stuck? Listen for the stories you'll hear.

When you hear a false narrative (and you will, all sorts of them), listen for the helplessness. Are you internally convinced that as soon as you finish the draft you won't know how to find or afford an editor? Choose to show your brain why you are *not* helpless. "Brain, I know you can't see right now how I'll know (or afford) what to do next, but we'll cross that bridge when we get there. What I *do* know is that I'm capable, resourceful, and smart. I've gotten this far using those very traits. When I get to the next obstacle, I may not know the solution, but I know how to take a single step toward one. I've got this." You can even go deeper if you're sensing you need it... and give your brain examples of what you'll do. "I know Marcy helps writers, so I'll contact her. See, Brain? We've got some great connections who will help us keep moving forward." You can do this through an actual conversation, letter writing, journaling, role-playing with a trusted friend, a doodle, whatever! As soon as your brain feels secure that you don't need to be stuck in a "freeze" state, you'll be released back into parts of your brain that allow you to move forward in the best possible ways.

Healing From Our Own Stories

Here's the thing: You can't share a story you haven't wrestled with. It doesn't matter if you're writing fiction or nonfiction... you have to work through your personal relationship with the stories you're telling.

You can try all the tips from this book, but without this piece, many of them won't work. That's why so many other books on this topic have great ideas but are ineffective for certain populations of writers: those of you trying to write your hard stories.

In order for your message to leave your heart, mind, and soul, you have to have made peace with it. You won't arrive at one hundred percent healing, but you'll have looked it in the face, felt the feels, made space for yourself to exist within the tragedies you've experienced, and taken the next step forward.

This is because your painful memories impact you in a couple of different ways. First, your brain is pain-avoidant. So, it certainly doesn't want to take you back to places of pain *again*. The problem is that unprocessed pain gets trapped in your brainstem. Unprocessed pain or trauma doesn't get filed away into a time or place in the brain's cataloging system. It will stay in the sensory part of your brain, your *always-present* brain. This is why a car backfiring can take a veteran immediately back to the battlefield... the brain has held those memories as unprocessed pain, with no assigned "home" in the brain like all of the other memories. So, when the car backfires, the brainstem responds with a deep belief that the person is *actually back in the battle*—not in the past, right now.

We easily recognize this in veterans but miss it in our own writing blocks. When you sit down to write about places of pain and injury, your brain over-reacts in an attempt to protect you from experiencing those moments again. To an extreme, we see the brain do this with dissociative identity disorder, where it actually splits off to protect itself from the trauma. In lesser extremes, we see this when sitting down to write a story you're not healed enough from when all of the pain-avoidant behaviors surface as, "Wow, those windows are filthy. I should clean them right this second. I'll write later."

The second way your painful memories impact your brain (and writing) is related to brain functions. Your Pre-Frontal Cortex (PFC) is your language center. This is the part of your brain primarily responsible for making meaning of language. When your nervous system is a bit activated because you're touching painful memories, the blood flow and oxygen *leave* your PFC and focus on your brainstem. Your brainstem, however, is not amazing with language at all. It's more like a caveman, grunting and gesturing to communicate its needs. Any story that is still held in some capacity in the brainstem *cannot* be communicated with words. We have to dislodge it, help the brain process it, and get that memory or experience filed away in the brain's cataloging system *before* words can be assigned to describe the meaning of it.

Have you ever been in a high-conflict situation and totally lost your words? Only *later* to think of all the amazing, clever, witty things you *should* have said? YES! This is because your brain shifted from your PFC to the direction of your brainstem, and you lost your ability to put words and meaning together.

The wonderful news is that one incredible way of dislodging unprocessed painful memories is through sensory activities, like fine arts, music, dance, and *writing*. Your brainstem loves *all that*. It enables your body to essentially tell the story before words become present. As you allow your body to express itself, uncensored, in one of these sensory activities, you engage healing.

"Now, Marcy, you just said *writing* is a healing sensory activity, but um... writing uses words. Soooo..."

Yes! I'm so glad you brought that up. Writing *uncensored* is a sensory activity. That means that when you free write, allowing your brain to dump anything it has inside, you begin a healing process. You may find that you don't have words to tell *that* story yet, and that's okay. Do a free writing exercise and see what comes out, whether or not it's related to the hard story you're eventually trying to get to. It may be that you have to clear the weeds from the topsoil of your brain before you can get to *that* story.

Now, by uncensored, I mean to allow yourself to write no matter how angry, offensive, uneducated, (fill in the blank) it needs to be. Many of us stop ourselves when we think, "Ooh, what if Aunt Betty were to read this." We change what we *would* have said, fearing the response of a person who might see it. In uncensored writing, we release those fears and put it *all* down. The good, the bad, and the ugly. If you don't normally swear but that's what's coming out... then let it out. If you don't normally express regret about something that might hurt someone... let it out. This is *for your eyes only.* You can burn it later. Edit it later. The important thing is that your body is allowed to say what it has been holding back. *That's where healing happens.*

Another factor in healing our hard places is to *allow* ourselves to venture back into the painful memory from the *safety* of the present. This requires an intentional effort to both remain grounded *and* free yourself to visit some of those painful experiences through your imagination. I often ask my therapy clients or workshop attendees to imagine their feet anchoring them to the ground. I ask them to feel their bodies in the seat, to feel the weight of their body holding them in this moment. Then I guide them through an activity that goes between writing and imagination. They carefully allow themselves to notice any memories that surface within the safety their body is experiencing in the sacred space of the room we share. Allowing our minds to relive traumatic moments while *actually being safe* in the present begins to shift how we remember the hard parts of our stories and where they live in our brain. I definitely recommend practices like this with a trained and specialized trauma and resilience therapist for our *really* painful stories. But for the purpose or working through your writing, there are a number of ways I encourage my authors to practice this process.

I ask my authors to make a list of "cushions" they can use to support their time writing their harder memories. There was a window of life when I experienced panic attacks. For us to have hard stories to write about, we had to *live them.* Well, this was a season of *living* one of my traumatic stories. I had a difficult Zoom conversation coming up and knew it could possibly trigger a panic attack. So, I chose to sit on the floor and surround myself with cushions. Actual cushions. One of the ways those panic attacks manifested for me was an intense feeling of about-to-pass-out. Therefore, I prepared my surroundings to support me. (Fortunately, that conversation *didn't* trigger an attack and I haven't had one for a while now. Yay!)

Sometimes we need *real* cushions to support us. And sometimes we need "cushions." Here are some "cushions" that I or my authors have used to have a supportive environment while writing the harder parts of their stories.

1. Play calming, supportive music before, during, and after you write (or some combination of these). Playing music before can calm your nervous system before even beginning. Playing music after can restore calm to your nervous system if it was activated during your writing time. And playing music *during* can be grounding, keeping some level of awareness that you are in *this* moment, and you are safe. I have a few playlists that I rotate between depending on what I need.
2. Tell a trusted friend that you're writing a hard part of your story and need them to "hold the rope." One of my best friends and I use this language and I love it. I imagine myself with a rope tied around my waist, with him safely holding the other end. This allows me to venture into my memories knowing a safe and caring person is holding me, ready to reel me back if I need it. Clearly, it's just my imagination, but it makes a difference in my ability to feel centered as I enter writing hard parts of my story. He "tugs" on the rope from time to time to see how I'm doing. And I let him know when I'm safely out of the writing pit. We even have emojis that say everything we need! Find a trusted friend and ask them to "hold the rope" for you. This can be through text or a phone call. If you want them to

"tug" on the rope and check in at a certain time, let them know the time and what you might need.

3. Schedule something fun or relaxing after your writing session. This will vary depending on how you're wired. For some, it's a guy's night out. For others, it's a soak in the bath with salts. You might find a long walk in nature restorative, or a trip to the gym! Whatever it is, be careful not to overestimate the energy you'll have after writing the hard parts of your story. Set an expectation that you can leave early if you need to or change plans altogether. You'll get a better sense of what you need as you get into writing the hard parts of your story. I love a night at home watching a good movie with my family or a good friend. I usually choose a lighter or funny movie to pull me up from any funk the writing left me in.

These are just a few examples to get you thinking about what *your* "cushions" might be. The options are as varied as human uniqueness. Find *your* thing and set it up all around you. Adjust as you learn and grow. Go slow, listen carefully to your body, and be patient and full of grace for yourself. The important thing is that you are showing your body that you *care,* that you see the wounded parts of yourself, and want to usher in healing. That you're willing to do the painful work of remembering in the safety of the present to heal and help others at the same time. This is a profound message to give your *whole* body.

It doesn't matter if you're writing for children or adults: THIS. IS. REAL.

There were places in my memoir, *While We Slept: Finding Hope and Healing After Homicide,* where even though I'd LIVED IT, I couldn't get the words out in an understandable way. I had to ask myself what was stopping me. Sometimes, that meant crying or forgiving myself or someone else—wrestling with my story until I felt peace. Sometimes it meant writing a chapter I wouldn't include in the book but needed to write for *myself*. The chapters where I talked about the pain caused by people I loved, which didn't ultimately need to be part of the published work but were nonetheless part of my writing journey. I had to write *that* chapter before I could write the *next* chapter. *Then* the words flowed... and one of the book's readers gave herself another chance to live because of my story.

> " *Marcy, I just finished reading your book. I've been in bed for months, deeply depressed and contemplating taking my own life. While reading your book I realized that if you could survive that, well, I can get out of bed and get dressed. Losing my husband of 40 years, my mild stroke earlier this year, and a big move left me vulnerable to some recent hurtful circumstances, which —after all—are* NOTHING *in the great scheme of things. I needed to read this message just when I did and be reminded that life is not over, but I can be strengthened and renewed in spirit, body, soul, and mind.*

When you do the work on your own healing in order to put your story into the world in the best possible way, you have no idea the impact it will have.

This was also true with my children's book, *Weirdo and Willy*, loosely based on a true story from my childhood. It took thirty-eight drafts of that story to get it right because I was still wrestling with my own childhood experience. I didn't realize it at the time, though. I thought I just couldn't get it right. It wasn't until an Amazon reviewer left a comment about how the bullies in the story never had a big repentant moment (she thought they should) that I began to see my own process with my story. My initial response to her review was, "Oh my goodness! She's right! How did I miss that? There's no big come-to-Jesus moment and there should've been! I know better!"

But then I stopped and thought about what my book actually taught. It taught that acceptance comes from *within.* That even if the bullies around you never change (in real life they rarely do), you hold agency over yourself to live a life of acceptance, friendship, and self-worth. My book teaches that our differences are cool, and that other people are weird too. Find your weird people and start a club.

Over the thirty-eight drafts, my book evolved from one of vengeance (a creature came and ate all of the bullies, bwahahaha!) to a story of unlikely friendship and unchanged bullies. Why? Because this was *my healing journey.* I moved *with* my story from a resentful hurt heart to a heart of peace and self-acceptance. This became the gift I now offer children. (It's a great book, you should read it.)

Now my readers are embracing their weirdness and forming healthy friendships, apart from the broken opinions of still-developing peers.

This happened with one of my clients, too.

Sasha was already a prolific writer. I had been her story and publishing coach, as well as her book editor, on a few of her books already. While she was writing the third book in her children's series, she got stuck and couldn't move forward. She was surprised because she'd previously been able to push through writer's block quite easily. She found herself in a new and upsetting situation of not knowing how to finish the book.

When we met and talked about her book, we discovered that her block was an unexpected connection to her childhood that was preventing her from being able to finish. In this particular book, her beloved main character, a dog, was being bullied at dog obedience school. Through coaching, she realized that she was feeling bad for the main character because she herself had been bullied as a child. She just couldn't internally, subconsciously, put her beloved character through the painful experiences she'd had as a child.

As we talked, and as this reality came to the surface, she began to cry and mourn her own childhood experience and really, really feel the pain of what she'd planned for her main character to experience in her book. I suggested a few ideas for how she could bring some peace to her own journey as a child who had been bullied, but also to her main character. We talked about writing her main character a letter to prepare her for what was coming in the story, which is what she did. Her letter let her character know that even though she would experience bullying from some of the other dogs at school, Sasha was very much in control of her story. She let her character know that this pain was temporary and purposed for good for kids in the world. She promised her character that it would only last a few pages before she would find her own strength and resilience through the pen of the author, as well as a new friendship. She also told her character that she wouldn't stay in a place of discomfort and pain.

My client wept during our call and her letter writing. As much as she needed her main character to know she was loved, cared for, seen, and not alone, my *author* needed to know the same for herself. While she was offering that kind of love and protection to her character, she was also offering that love and protection to the little girl inside of her who still felt so wounded from her own early years of bullying. This released her to finish the book.

When she gave me the next draft of her book, which was essentially the first draft, it was the best first draft I've ever been given; it was so well written. I saw how doing the healing work with her own childhood story and connecting that to the blockage that was preventing her from finishing released her creativity and helped her to do the very thing that she most wanted to do—give the world a story in which kids could understand the pain of bullying but also be equipped and empowered to withstand it. To come out stronger, not defined by the words or actions of bullies, but instead by the confidence and belief that they could have within themselves. This was a powerful experience.

Pro Tip: If you're staring at a blank screen or bored by your own writing, pause. Ask yourself, "What areas of my heart still need a little attention? What can I do to dislodge my unprocessed pain?" Consider grabbing some Play-Doh and letting your hands create. Don't plan it, script it, or think about it, just mold the Play-Doh into *something*. When you feel complete, hold that thing in your hand. Ask your creation, "What would you like me to know?" and listen. You can journal the thoughts that come to mind or speak them out loud to yourself as they come to you. Bring your curiosity to your creation. If you see something you don't understand, ask about it. "What's the little bumpy part right here? Tell me about that," and notice what you hear.

Then allow yourself to respond. What do *you* want your creation to know? You can go back and forth as many times as you'd like until you and your creation both feel heard. This is a surprisingly simple yet powerful sensory activity that can begin healing the parts of your wounded heart that need attention.

You can also create a collage, draw or paint a picture, beat on a drum (or drum-like thing), or move your body the way it wants to move (remember, uncensored!). Then try writing again and see if anything has shifted!

Fear of Others

Some of our greatest fears stem from what others will think about us. We're afraid they'll see us for who we "really" are and we'll be outed, that they'll think too highly of us and we'll disappoint them, or that they'll have a negative response to something we worked so hard to create.

This is the foundation for imposter syndrome, a belief that you are a fraud somehow successfully masquerading among people who are better than you. With that belief comes a fear that someone will discover the charade and the party will be over—you'll be back on the streets where you probably belong, with the lesser-than-everyone-else crowd. The reality is, just about *everyone* feels this way, even many global leaders, diplomats, celebrities, parents, educators, and influencers.

Let's address a few of the most common ways the fear of others shows up.

1. Fear of their opinion.

As we discussed in previous sections, our fears are often attached to a meaning we've assigned to them—a story we've told ourselves and have believed. A fear of others and their opinions often reveals a belief we hold that someone else's opinion is somehow a reflection of our worth. If someone doesn't like my book, then I must be a horrible writer (and therefore a fraud or imposter). And if I'm a horrible writer... then what? What comes next? So, what if I *am* a horrible author? What does that mean for me/about me? If I listened closely, I might hear something like, "If I'm a horrible author (based on a negative review) then I've been a fool and exposed myself to the world. Everyone will know that I thought more of myself than I am. I'll be embarrassed. I'll need to hide from everyone. Only losers don't know their place. It's safer if I just *don't*."

Here's a truth bomb: every amazing writer you've read had a team of people get their book to that shelf. Their first draft was just as shoddy as yours, maybe worse. They battled all the same blocks and messages and fears, but they pressed on. They invited beta readers, editors, publishers... a whole slew of people to their team to help them make it the best possible book it could be. Some editors all but re-write the author's book (that's not my approach, but it happens out in the wild!). There are extremely well-known books I could name (but I'll spare the authors) whose *published books* still had copy errors and plot holes, only to be pulled back, fixed even *more*, and republished. Do *not* compare your draft to the books you see on the shelves. It's not a fair comparison by a million miles. Compare your draft to the draft before it. Compare it to the blank page it used to be.

And when the day comes that you put the pages of your blood, sweat, and tears in a book on a shelf (digital or otherwise) and someone doesn't *like it*, then guess what? You just learned who your audience *isn't*. There *will* be people who love it. There will be people who like it. And there will be a few who don't. Learn what you can from their review (if anything) and release the rest to the unique life experience of that person and the disparity between their expectations and your target reader. *No single book in creation has ever been loved by everyone.* And yours won't either.

This brings us to your identity. Make sure it is grounded in something beyond your achievements. Make sure it's grounded in something beyond the opinions of other in-process people.

My friend Gary Williams changed my life with the following imagery. One day, he mentioned the workout structures in many of Michigan's parks. It was a nice day and he'd gone for a run, pausing to use some of this free equipment. I knew he also held a gym membership. "Why do you pay for a membership when you can just go to the park for a workout?" I asked.

He reminded me that parks in Michigan are under feet of snow in the winter. Oh, yeah!

"Thanks for holding up that mirror, Gary. I should've known better. Of *course* you can't work out with under-snow equipment." I shook my head at my own mindlessness. I know Michigan has snowy winters.

"*Marcy*," he replied. "That's not a mirror, that's a window. Why would you know what a Michigan park is like in the winter? You're in California! I let you peek through a *window* into my own experience."

I think I just sat there stunned for a minute. My mind flashed through all the years of my life leading up to that very moment—the endless amount of times I'd lived as if someone was holding up a mirror. In fact, I didn't know windows existed. It took Gary audibly saying, "That's not a mirror, that's a window," to get me to realize how many times I'd misidentified the object.

Now I realize how few people actually have the right or power to hold up a mirror for me. First, I personally look to God for my most accurate reflection. Next, I allow a few trusted friends in my inner circle to hold up mirrors (and even then, because they're human, I have to bring my own wisdom and discernment to the interactions). Thank God for friends like Gary.

Sometimes people try to convince me that their words are a mirror for me. These tend to be, in actuality, some of the biggest windows. Even so, sometimes I'll take what they're calling a mirror and share it with my trusted friends and take it to prayer. I know they'll give me honesty because they love me and want to see me grow, be healthy, and be connected. Those are the people I've chosen to be close to me. They'll help me discern whether the other person's object is a mirror or a window.

So, here's what I want you to know about the mirrors and windows in your life. Most of them are windows. Book reviews tend to be windows. Feedback from family and friends is often a window. That reviewer is allowing you to peek through their window into their life experience, personality, or level of development and maturity. Does my heart still pound like a racehorse when I see a negative review? Absolutely! My old belief that everything is a mirror still flashes for a millisecond, fighting for my attention and affection. But "Nope!" I say, "not today!" I allow myself some distance from the words, take deep breaths, and center myself on what's true.

When I feel grounded, I return to the review and consider what's helpful to me and what isn't. Is there something genuine that I can improve? Does my book description mislead people about the content of my book? Have I unintentionally attracted the wrong audience? What can I improve so the right people find my book? Is there something I can improve about the book's content? Maybe. More times than not, the person holds up a window to what they're looking for. One negative reviewer let me peek through her window into a worldview that demanded foster and adoptive parents say that raising children of trauma is easy, everyone should do it, and you don't need Jesus to do it! "Good luck finding that book!" I said to the review, closing the tab and grateful to have recognized a window from a mirror. In the past, I would have been mortified, positive that I'd failed at serving the foster-adopt community, that somehow, I'd injured people who were already hurting, and how dare I mention my faith! I might have even been tempted to pull it (I once deleted an entire blog because *one person* didn't like what I wrote about an experience we'd shared). That foster-adoption book continues to be one of my best-selling, most-loved books by readers around the world. The one reviewer held up a window, not a mirror.

Sometimes it's not the reviewer, but a family member or "friend." *Sometimes*, the people with the most access to us feel entitled to hold up a mirror. They might say things like, "What, you? Write a book! HA!" Or they might say, "That's awesome! I'm in your corner. You can totally write a book; I believe in you" (keep *these* people). Anyone encouraging your dream is still holding up a window... they're revealing their character and belief.

I can't tell you how many of my clients have been told by someone (and often multiple someones) that they aren't good enough to achieve their dream. They've been told they're too dumb, too slow, too technologically illiterate, too boring, or not enough—not good enough, skilled enough, exciting enough, young enough, old enough, just... not enough. More windows.

You know how when someone starts to lose weight, people around them get antsy? The person changing their body is also changing the dynamics that have been at play. Some people feel threatened by the weight loss of their friend or family member... what if that person becomes more beautiful? Thinner than everyone else? More desired? What if their weight loss makes me feel bad about *myself*? Sometimes people will try to discourage you and thwart you on your way to your dream because it threatens *them*. That is *not* your responsibility. That's a window.

If a voice in your life is trying to diminish your dream, take a beat and look through that window. What do you see? Have they pursued their own dreams? Do they regularly feel threatened by change? By the success of others? What does that reveal about where they are on their life journey? What of that is your job to take care of? Bring your curiosity to their window but stay on your side of it. Show up as a witness... but don't crawl through. That's not a playground you want to play on. Stay on your side of the window, learn what you can about that person, then get back to slaying your goals.

A fear of someone's opinion is a fear that you'll find yourself worthless. Friend, don't give anyone that power. Your worth is entirely separate from someone's opinion.

2. Fear of Retribution

Sometimes when we're telling our hard stories, especially our true stories, we have a justifiable fear of retribution. I've had several clients with people in prison who committed the crimes their book is about, or people who *should be* in prison but aren't because they weren't convicted for the crimes they committed. Some clients are telling never-before-told stories that some family members would prefer to remain in the closet. Some very well-meaning people might even tell you that the most respectful, thoughtful, kind thing you can do is withhold your story if *everyone who has an opinion about it* isn't one hundred percent on board.

I've had some clients move from fear of retribution into the experience *of* retribution. One of my authors published a book about her experience in an abusive marriage. Her book was about her escape and inspiration and encouragement to others who were stuck in abusive homes. She used pseudonyms and did what she could to get her story into the hands of other victims. But her abuser and his family found out and began leaving comments and reviews wherever they could. They weren't discreet (and they weren't smart). They gave themselves away, but they were still loud. And they were still abusive. She ended up unpublishing her book and taking another year or two to get herself set up and ready to try again. And she did! Not only is her book revised and on shelves, but she's started an entire company helping marital abuse victims get out and get safe. So, at first read, it may seem like her abusers won... she pulled her book. But in the pulling of her book (which could have felt like a failure), she re-grouped, learned a ton, and came back with a backbone of steel and conviction and confidence to match. Well, and a lawyer.

Retribution is real and you won't find it minimized here. With that said, there's still room to weigh fear against reality. Sometimes our fear is heightened and enhanced. Sometimes it's an appropriate caution sign. One way to know for sure, in your case, is to contact a lawyer. That's what I did with my memoir, *While We Slept*. That's when I learned that some states, like mine, have a slap statute that protects authors from frivolous claims. Certain laws give us the freedom to share our truth. Certain disclaimers have been held up in court to protect your right to share your story. Even so, my lawyer asked me to weigh my legal rights against the relational impact. What may be legal may not be beneficial. Each author has to consider this with deep regard. Do your due diligence. Stay safe. Honor your story.

At the same time, many victims have been silenced for so long that we're terrified of using our voices and "getting into trouble." Some victims will even take on the behavior of their abuser and *self*-silence, further cutting off their important message from a world desperate for it. We self-censor, holding back voices that need to be heard *and* preventing our healing. Remember what I said about censorship and our healing? When we can self-express unscripted and freely, we make space for healing. That doesn't mean we need to make all of our healing work public. It does mean that when we engage our sensory activity of writing, and we allow self-censoring in the initial draft, we are working against our healing.

I encourage my memoir writers to let their first draft be raw and real. It's not the draft that will be published. But it's the draft they need to write to ever get to the draft they can share. You will cut out what your audience doesn't need later, add what they *do* need that you didn't write before, and give the world a polished, appropriate, important, revised version of your book once you've done your work. So, when the fear of retribution comes up in the first draft... put it aside. You will come back to that once you've got words to work with and an ideal reader to serve.

I still have to weigh all of this each time I share on a podcast, a guest blog, or in my own books. I have many stories that involve the inappropriate and unacceptable behavior of others, and even if my goal is only to share my part in it... theirs is unavoidable to some degree. I always use my audience as the filter... what do they need from me? What's too much? What's not enough? Like Goldilocks, I want to give my reader "just right." I also have to check my own heart. Am I writing to get back at someone? Am I writing from a place of unhealthy, unmanaged anger? Am I writing because I love other humans and want to help them with my story? Essentially, am I writing from a place of love (for myself and/or others) or anger? When I catch anger, I slow down and step back. I haven't experienced anything good coming from a root of anger. This makes a tremendous difference for me in how, where, and when I show up with my story.

3. Fear of Idolization

Similar to a fear of success, we can sometimes become afraid of becoming too well-known or popular, of being put on a pedestal. I'm so aware that I don't know everything there is to know on a topic. So, what if something I write does well and people assume I know *all the things*? Cue more imposter syndrome. Or what if people begin to think highly of me and I can't live up to their expectations? This is a big stress point for me for a few reasons.

A. I'm an introvert. My energy is limited, and I have to budget it wisely. I have a fear of being too needed and not having enough to give. I worry that I'll end up exhausted and depleted (I "expired" once, you can read about that elsewhere). I've sometimes caught myself keeping myself small, insignificant, and under the radar just to preserve my energy. You don't have to be introverted to budget your time and energy. We all have an allotted amount to give, some of us more than others. Burnout isn't only for the introverted. Those of us who feel aware of our limitations might find ourselves fearing the idolization of others.

B. I hate disappointing people. If I follow that thought beneath the hood, I find a belief that disappointing people is the fastest path to proving to everyone that you're not worth loving. (This is false, of course, and a belief I'm reframing as we speak). But I still hate disappointing people. And when they think "too" highly of me, I start to panic. It's a looooong drop from the top and I'm not in for it. There's both health and dysfunction here for me, humility and pride. Guess what? I'm going to disappoint people, and so are you. Disappointment is often more about the other person's expectations than our worth or ability to *not* disappoint. It's another window, not a mirror. Fearing disappointing people is my personal quickest way to paralysis so I have to stay on top of this as a false belief.

C. I value individuation. I love the uniqueness of each person. In fact, seeing people as individuals is a strength of mine! It also means I get really uncomfortable if it's not clear that any achievement I've accomplished was a team effort. A whole group of people helped me get on the TEDx stage twice. Another whole group has helped me get each of my books onto shelves. It's taken a community to help me raise my children. There's literally nothing in my life (I believe) that has occurred without the love, support, encouragement, and guidance of someone right next to me. Sometimes I'm the face plastered on the promotional image, and sometimes it's someone I've had the privilege of championing. When I'm elevated to a high status in someone's mind, I'm tempted to worry that everyone who got me there is somehow minimized, missed, or diminished in some way (something I've painfully experienced my whole life and want no one else to ever experience). This all sounds noble, right? Some of it is. And some of it is my fear of the spotlight, of being exposed. My survival skills in life (and the form of abuse I experienced) were primarily around being small, hidden, and away from attention. This feels safe—and it keeps my dreams small. I have to regularly check in with myself and ask if I'm fearing idolization from a place of wanting others to have their just recognition *or* as a deflection so I can hide behind my people to feel safe.

Maybe you've had this fear as well, a fear of being held up too high in the regard of others. It's not something we talk about very much. In fact, our culture would convince us that this is what we want! To be *numero uno* standing on the highest pinnacle of any award platform. Some of us sabotage our own work and dreams to keep us exactly from that position.

Pro Tip: I mention it above, but it's worth adding here too. Gather a trusted group of champions and keep them close. Community is one of the most healing agents of change. As I said before, your brain perceives a threat to survival through a lens of physical safety *and* emotional safety. Guess what begins to heal emotional safety? Belonging, community, and connection. Many of us with emotional wounds and blocks got them *from* people, some from individuals and some from communities. It can be hard to feel safe with people; I get it. That's why this is a pro tip. Find your people. Vet them (not just anyone is allowed that privileged seat). Start with one and go from there. Find safe, trusted communities if you need one to get started (this might be a focus group around the kind of emotional or relational injury you experienced. There are groups for victims of abuse and crimes, divorce groups, parenting groups, singles groups, addiction, veteran's groups, and on and on). Find a belonging space and *be* a belonging space. This will help you navigate the opinions of others, determine windows from mirrors, and initiate an important salve to your relational injuries.

Fear of the Goodbye/Closure

In all of my years of interacting with and coaching writers, this one only just recently came to my attention. And yep, it was during a recent coaching call.

My client was finishing up the third middle-grade book in her trilogy. I was her coach and editor, so I knew her stories intimately. She only needed to finish the last few chapters but was experiencing writer's block and couldn't finish. When we met, she mentioned that she kept missing her deadlines (which I was well aware of). She had some reasons—life—but didn't have real strong clarity on why she was *really* stuck. Again, she'd written so many other books and this one was really hanging her up.

During the writing of this third book, her father passed away unexpectedly. As we were talking about putting together a strategic plan for finishing this book by a new deadline, she began to grieve the passing of her father. She felt how his passing had impacted her ability to sit down and write. As she was processing that, she said, "And when I finish this book, I'll feel like I'm saying goodbye to him *again*."

And *boom* there it was.

Through her ability to process the grief of her father's passing, she unlocked the actual blockage between her finishing those last few chapters. Her books include the relationship between a little girl and her father as a subplot in the greater story. She had written her sweet relationship with her dad into the story. With him now gone, she could feel so acutely that when she ended the series, she would have to face the silence of her dad's absence. Recognizing that enabled us to look at alternative ways of viewing her relationship with her dad and her relationship with her book.

Instead of seeing the end of this third book as the end of a relationship with the trilogy, or the end of getting to sit with her daddy as she wrote out this beautiful story, we shifted her thinking toward new beginnings. Instead of this being an end, it would be a pivot. Instead of sitting and writing with her dad, she'd continue to spend time with him as she promoted it, as she stood at a booth at author events, or shared with classrooms of children on school visits. Her dad would be with her for every moment.

I watched the shift happen right in front of me. She found herself excited again and relieved—this was just the end of *one way* of spending time together. Once we shifted her thinking here, her mind opened to even more possibilities! She said, "Well, I have another book planned, not connected to this series, but one that also looks at the relationship between a father and daughter."

Well, there you have it. This is the beauty of a brain dislodging blocks. It's like a dam, once you remove the obstacle to the flow, it pours.

Once she acknowledged her fear of the goodbye, she was able to offer alternative messages that better supported her, which were still true! That enabled her to put her gift out to the world. Not with the sadness of closure and loss but instead with the excitement of a new chapter and new ways to spend time with her late daddy.

There are other goodbyes we struggle with as well.

I have another client who's been working on her book for over thirty years. Good thing she found me! We can finally get that baby published! On a recent call, she broke into tears as she thought about handing her book to me for editing. "Marcy, this book has been with me for *so* long. What will I do with myself once it's done?" This was a powerful and important moment. She was able to get beneath the hood and feel the fear of closure that was keeping her from finishing her book! This opened up opportunities for us to talk about launching her baby from the nest and making space for new babies! She admitted she had other book ideas she'd love to write. Once we got her excited for her next book babies, she was able to imagine letting this first one go. And just like the client I mentioned above, this author would *always* have her book, it would just be a graduated version.

Pro Tip: For some people, reframing thoughts around endings and beginnings can be really helpful. Others of us need to sit with the feels and honor them before moving on. We do this with graduations, weddings, and funerals—we make space and time to honor, celebrate, and remember. Do this with your book! Have a book launch party where you pause to celebrate the "graduation" of your book from the nest to the world! Not only does it provide an opportunity to announce and sell your book, gather people, and throw a party, but it allows you to embody and experience a very important "rite of passage" for your book. This can help your brain make peace with the change and open up to new possibilities.

CHAPTER ELEVEN

emotional blocks

GRAB THE WRENCH

GRAB THE WRENCH

It's that time again! Grab the wrench and get beneath the hood! Review the pro tips and see which one most resonates with you. Sit with your feelings, beliefs, and the assigned messages. Get beneath the surface as soon as your "check engine" light comes up. And get to work! Your book matters! Don't let these sneaky emotional blocks trip you up. Remember, they look like pebbles but trip you up like stones... until you make them the steppingstone that they *can* be.

If you find yourself in a fight-or-flight state, do something calming and grounding. Take a break and dig your toes into the dirt, grass, or ocean (whatever you have access to!). Feel the breeze, take in the sounds around you, or get a massage. Drink some water, go for a walk, or ask for a hug from a loved one. Do something that tells your physical body that you're safe. Once your nervous system has deactivated, you can try returning to your writing.

And give yourself "cushions!" That means that if you know you're going to be working on a harder part of your story, something connected to your own injury or painful experience, plan around it! Schedule some friend time later in the day, get candles and bath salts ready for a nice bath, or ask a friend to call and check in on you. Whatever is life-giving and restorative to you—plan it. That way you're not left alone with a potentially activated nervous system. Take care of yourself... writing is *not* for the faint of heart!

CHAPTER TWELVE

emotional blocks

BACK ON THE ROAD

GET BACK ON THE ROAD

EMOTIONAL BLOCKS CAN BE some of the hardest to overcome. They sneak up in some way in most of the blocks we experience. Because we are emotional beings, our perceptions are often fueled by our feelings, which turns the rudder on our ship and sends us in a direction. If you're only reactive, you'll become a slave to the rudder and the direction it takes you. If you're responsive, you can pause and ask good questions, challenge your limiting beliefs, and shape your perception, thus taking control of the wheel and steering toward your dream.

Emotional blocks have derailed you for too long. It's time to get back on the road. Now let's dive into our next block.

scarcity blocks

"One of the pieces I'm deeply proud to have written started with a paragraph that read: 'This story needed an ending before it could find its first sentence. So please forgive me for delivering it ten years overdue.' That ten years was a war with writer's block."

—Cal Fussman

CHAPTER THIRTEEN

scarcity blocks

THE GEEK OUT

In this section, we're going to talk about scarcity blocks. It's important to understand that anytime we perceive a lack in our life, we will also experience some kind of block. The types of scarcity we might experience include a scarcity of time, a scarcity of money, and a scarcity of any resource, including creativity, knowledge, motivation, and self-awareness. Our perception of security can show up in many different places. We're going to talk about some of those in this section.

Now let's recall what we've learned so far about the brain. Hopefully, by now, if I started a call and response cheer like this: "What do our brains want?!" You'd be able to finish with, "Survival!"

"What kind of survival?!"

"Physical and emotional!"

Wow! Look at us! We'd make an awesome cheer squad.

We covered some of the emotional threats to safety and security in our previous section. In this section, we're going to look at both physical *and* emotional threats to safety and survival through the lens of scarcity.

THE GEEK OUT

When your brain experiences a lack, it immediately enters a mode of solving for the lack. Your brain wants to make sure all of your basic needs are met. As we see in Maslow's hierarchy, there's a prioritization that happens in your mind and body related to meeting your needs. First, from a very basic primal level, and then all the way through the self-actualization (becoming the best version of yourself) level.

These types of needs can experience lack and create a block in our creativity. When your brain experiences a perceived lack, it is tempted to enter into the freeze state of your survival response. If you are not aware of the resources you have available to you to address that lack, you can feel helpless and hopeless.

When you experience helplessness or hopelessness, you become paralyzed.

Think of a wild animal out in nature. If a predator comes against it, the brain does an impressively fast scan of the situation. Which is most likely to lead to survival? Running? Fighting? Trying to please the predator? Playing dead? The brain will immediately cycle through all of the options and resources available in order to potentially win the conflict or the battle against the oppressor.

Let's say that in that quick scan, the brain determines that there aren't enough resources to ensure survival by fighting the bad guy. In this case, it will resort to the flight mode. If in another quick scan, it's determined that there's no way to escape and survive, the brain will then shift into a freeze.

One of the most obvious images of a freeze state is a deer standing in the middle of the road while a car is coming toward it. Its brain quickly tries to process, *Can I fight this obstacle? Can I run from this obstacle?* While the brain is trying to sort through all of the resources available for survival, the deer remains frozen in the middle of the road. Unfortunately, this ultimately leads to the death of many deer. This is where we get the saying, "He was like a deer in headlights."

Well, this happens inside our brains too. The difference is that our main predator isn't a car on a road, though we do need to be careful. It's not always a physical threat to our physical body, in the sense of some kind of battle that we might have to win. Your brain is constantly scanning your environment for cues of physical and emotional safety and threats. Based on what it finds in that scan your brain then looks for resources to combat the threat and secure safety.

That is the essence of resilience! When you experienced conflict in the past and overcame that experience, it built upon itself. You showed your brain and body what you're capable of, whether you keep your promises to yourself or whether you don't, the tools that have worked for you and the ones that haven't. I love resilience, but it's often misunderstood and incorrectly taught. That's why I speak about resilience in both of my TEDx talks... it's important to understand how it develops so we can have appropriate expectations for children and get more of it!

The beautiful thing about your brain is that it's constantly trying to add to your toolbox of resources. It wants to solve your scarcity block by showing you your access to provision. Again, you have to consider your thought life, the beliefs that you've taken on, and the meaning you've assigned to those beliefs in order to challenge your brain's perception of the resources you have and your ability to conquer your scarcity block.

CHAPTER FOURTEEN

scarcity blocks

THE CHECK ENGINE LIGHT

ENGINE CHECK

When your brain falls into a freeze state because you think that you're helpless to solve your problem, you end up paralyzed.

This is where your brain completely empties of any ideas. You might even feel your eyes widen. When you think about sitting down to write, the problems seem insurmountable. You're stuck staring into the headlights of an oncoming threat (which in this case is writing your story!).

What if you could reframe your perceptions of scarcity into that of limitless access and permission instead? This would free you from a scarcity block. It would unleash your creativity onto your page.

When your brain is in a freeze state, there are other symptoms you may notice as well.

1. You'll have trouble accessing the language center of your brain, struggling to put words to your experience.
2. You may have trouble concentrating.

3. Your mouth might feel dry.
4. You'll notice feelings of helplessness and defeat.
5. You may notice anxiety and varying degrees of panic.
6. You may notice that your sleep is a bit disrupted.
7. You're easily agitated and less patient.
8. You might notice that your palms are clammy or sweaty.
9. Your teeth may begin to chatter as though you're *actually* freezing, leading to trembling in other areas of your body as well.
10. You may feel light-headed or dizzy.

Some of these may seem similar to the symptoms we found with mental blocks as well.

This is your brain function!

Now let's get beneath the hood.

CHAPTER FIFTEEN

scarcity blocks

BENEATH THE HOOD

BENEATH THE HOOD

A PERCEPTION that you don't have enough time or energy or resources to complete your publishing project communicates to your brain that you are helpless, that you cannot overcome this problem, and that you're wasting the very few resources you *do* have on something that you won't be able to complete. We can choose to live with a scarcity mentality or a growth mentality.

A scarcity mentality believes that there are limited amounts of resources in the world, therefore what you *do* have must be hoarded. A growth mentality perceives an abundance of resources in the world, enough for everyone and enough for you. It's a matter of leaning into what you already have in order to expand what's available to you. Our survival mode focuses on a scarcity mentality. Shift from believing that you don't have what you need to complete your project, and enter the healthier, more supportive parts of your brain that are on fire and ready to get your books written and published, and into the hands of the people you care about.

Let's look at forms of scarcity that live beneath the hood.

Scarcity of Time

Over my years of coaching, I've heard, on countless occasions, people use the excuse, "I just don't have time." When they've missed deadlines, targets, or goals, they come with the excuse, "I've been too busy." It's true that we have a limited number of hours in any given day, and that we need to allocate and budget the use of those hours. Many of us have more going on in life than just this writing project. Maybe you are raising children or have a full-time job or parents that you're caring for.

I can't tell you how many people have said, "I'll write and publish when I retire," only to find that the retired life is just as full and busy and robust as the life of parents of young children. Maybe you're scraping by, taking every opportunity for income just to pay your bills. Yes, it's easy to look at all of these actual time suckers and accuse them of why the book is not getting done.

When your brain perceives a lack of time, it quickly scans your internal and external resources to determine what can be done about this lack of time. It also scans your motivation, wading through all of your beliefs about this particular lack of time, the meaning that's been assigned to having a lack of time, and your experiences overcoming a lack of time in your past. If it lands on, "Nope, nothing I can do about that!" you find yourself blocked.

If we dig deeper and get beneath the hood, we see that the belief that we don't have enough time has meaning attached to it. For some people, not having enough time is an easy deflection from some of the greater fears or insecurities we've already discussed. It appears to be a justifiable and valid excuse. It's hard to argue with because we all know that our time is actually limited. But I've also known people to realize that a scarcity of time is really a need for an adjustment to the time budget.

One of my authors was committed to getting her book done. She was a busy mom and employee, a wife, and had lots of things going on in her life. Looking at her calendar, we could both see that it was true—there was a lot vying for her attention and time. It would have been easy for her to say, "Well, I guess this isn't the season of life to write and publish the book I care so much about." Many authors have done just that. Some of them never publish their books at all. But this author was committed to getting up at 4 a.m. to work on her story before her day began at 5:30.

You need to know that this client was not a morning person. The idea of getting up at 4 a.m. was almost revolting to her. And I'll be honest, that's a different level of commitment than I've shown any of my books! I'll more easily skip a meal or cancel events or withdraw from commitments than I will get up at 4 a.m. and hope my brain will function to write. But this client found that this was a window of time that she could try. That's exactly how she went into it: "I'm going to try. I'm going to give it a week and see how it impacts my energy throughout the day. I'm going to see how my brain functions at 4 a.m. Because it really matters to me that this gets get out." And so, she did. She ended up writing and publishing her book by getting up every morning at 4 a.m. Her story inspires me, even though I was her coach. It shows me that when we care about what we're doing, we *will* make the sacrifices of time that need to be made. We all have the same twenty-four hours to work with. You get to decide which of those hours go where. Yes, that might mean that you need to say no for a short period of time while you prioritize your book.

Show your brain that it's not a *scarcity* of time but rather an *invitation* to reprioritize how the time you're given is used. Maybe it's not a 4 a.m. wake-up for you. But maybe it's telling your whole family that between this hour and that hour, you are to be uninterrupted so you can focus on your project. Maybe it means turning off your notifications when you're inside of your scheduled writing time to make sure you're not distracted.

There are a number of resources for helping prioritize and manage your time. Gary Williams is not only my good friend but also my strategy and productivity coach who helps me prioritize how I'm going to spend my hours in the coming week. I also meet with him to prioritize each quarter and each year. I don't have that skill naturally. I struggle to prioritize things correctly. So, for me, that has meant inviting accountability to keep me on track. It's because of his coaching that this book is even getting completed (for reals). If you need that support too, reach out to someone like Gary.

Do an honest self-assessment around the time you have and how you're actually using it, then present those resources to your brain. Show yourself that you are not in a *lack* but rather have an opportunity to respond to an invitation.

Pro Tip: This is an opportunity to remember why you are writing your book. It's very hard to overcome any block but specifically blocks that take you to a freeze state. We've talked about this before, but it's worth saying again—know who you are writing for and how you hope to impact them. Are you writing for children? Then picture those children, picture their lives without your book. Picture your life before you found your favorite most impactful book. Don't withhold that from them by nursing a misunderstanding around your access to time. Give your story to the world.

Are you writing for adults? What is it you hope they'll gain from your experiences? Or your wisdom? Or the opportunity to escape into your fictional world? What's their life like while they're waiting for your book? What kind of pain are they sitting in not knowing that you hold the keys to something better? When you're confronted with a lack of time, but you remember why this is so important for you and your ideal readers, you will fight to overcome any obstacle in your way to get that cure into their hands and hearts.

Scarcity of Money

Now let's talk about our perceived lack of money. I grew up on welfare, sometimes in a single-parent home. I didn't know any better. We got free food at distribution centers when it was offered. There were days we didn't know where our next meal was coming from. Suddenly, someone would knock on a door and a church group would be there, dropping off food right when we needed it. I grew up with the idea that my physical resources were limited, that they often came in the final hour but with a lot of stress and anxiety and questioning. My mom did an incredible job trying to protect us from *her* stress and anxiety around our limited financial means. But still, kids sense things. As a result, I took on the belief that the more I could provide, even as a young child, for my own family, the better off we were. This developed a deeper belief in me that financial security requires multiple people's contributions, that resources are scarce, and that we must hoard what we have. And that money somehow is for *other* people and not for me. Granted, I didn't know I had any of these beliefs until I was in a business building seminar. One of the sessions was specifically around our relationship with money. Through a questionnaire and interview, I was confronted with these deeply ingrained beliefs I held about money. I also learned that those beliefs caused me to sabotage my experiences with money.

Because of my belief that money was scarce, I kept what I had and never learned to invest in things that might actually increase my money. Anything that felt risky was avoided. When it came time to write and publish or to build my business, I learned that the only way to increase my income was to increase my financial investment. That was terrifying. It took a lot of prayer, faith, some epiphanies I believe God gave me, and really sitting and looking at my money beliefs before I handed over my first $500 to a writing and publishing program. I felt selfish. I was afraid I had just wasted money that my family could have used. I was doubtful that I could be one of the successful people in the program.

But I did it. I handed over that $500. That $500 became the seed of what would be my very first book, which immediately opened doors of opportunity for me to speak at retreats and conferences, and eventually on multiple TEDx stages. That $500 ended up being the seed money that led to the business I currently run. Had I in my fear withheld that money to keep it safe from all of the risks, I would still only have that $500. I wouldn't have my business, I wouldn't have my books, and I wouldn't have the thousands of people I've been able to impact through my coaching and my own storytelling. You wouldn't be holding this book. Wow! I feel the emotion of it even as I write. I'm so grateful for the people who gave me eyes to see how faulty my beliefs were around money.

Obviously, publishing *costs*. Whether you go a traditional route or a self-publishing route, you will have costs, they just get charged at different times in the process. A self-published author is going to have upfront costs. A traditionally published author is going to have back-end costs. What does that mean? It means that when you are acquired by a traditional publisher, they fronted the money for you, and cover your upfront costs with the belief that your book is going to make back the money they spent on you. Generally, you don't get royalty checks until the money they spent on you is paid off through the sales of your book. You still pay your own publishing costs.

Yet, I'm constantly amazed at how many people come to me wanting to write and publish with no clue of the costs that are associated with publishing. Even in my own business where I offer Done-For-You and Done-With-You publishing services, people are surprised at the cost of book production. If you don't have the skill yourself, you'll need to hire a cover designer so that your book looks professional and attracts your target audience. That saying, "Don't judge a book by its cover" has misled us for generations. We judge books by their covers! A cover will make or break your book. A cover design can cost hundreds of dollars. You're not just paying for the time of that person who's designing your cover, you're paying for their education, their years of developing the skill you're using, the cost of the tools they use to create your cover, etc. Their time is worth it alone. But remember, whenever you hire someone to support the production of your book, you're not *only* paying for their time.

You need a book formatter—someone who can take your text and turn it into the files that you need for publishing. If you can't do that, you will be paying money to somebody who can. You will hire an editor. Even though I *am* an editor, I still hire other editors for my own work. We need other sets of eyes looking at our books. We need somebody who has some distance from our work and knowledge to help develop our stories to the best possible version of themselves and make sure that it looks professional, and that all of our grammar is correct. Publishing an unedited book will lead to reviewers making comments on how poorly written and edited the book is. It doesn't matter if you're writing a 500-word children's picture book or a 100,000-word young adult book—editing matters, and you will pay somebody to do that for you.

Well, now that you've heard *some* of the costs associated with publishing, you're probably positive that you have a lack of money. I encourage you to challenge your beliefs around money just like I had to do. Open yourself to the possibility of finding the money you need to get this project into the world. There are definitely ways to cut costs. Sometimes that's hiring someone to help you. You can save time, energy, and money by letting someone do the work for you. There's a misconception that a DIY book production will save you money, but in the long run, if your book doesn't look professional, it won't *make* money. So once again, the more you invest, the more you should potentially get back from it.

Okay, so maybe you have a limited income. I have a number of retired clients with fixed incomes. And yet they're hiring my services. How can that be? So many of us have jobs with scalable or expendable income, but still hold a belief that we don't have enough, that we lack what we need. There are insightful studies in the world that show that an increase in money doesn't actually lead to an increase in happiness. It might lead to an increase of stuff, but you'll simply use the money you have, no matter how much you have, and it will always feel insufficient—unless you change your perception of money and work through your relationship with money.

The last time I had a client say to me, "Marcy, I've made it this far with my book; I've paid the illustrator, but now I need to buy the ISBN numbers. My rent was late last month and I'm still trying to catch up on other bills I missed. I just don't have the money to buy my ISBN." Well, the fact may be that you don't actually have the dollars in your bank account. But if you leave your brain there to believe that this equals "not enough" or lack or scarcity, it will struggle to find the resources you need to solve that problem. All of us have an opportunity to find or make money. Maybe this means you take on a freelance gig for a time, where you contract a skill you have to cover your costs. Many authors I know have had very successful crowdfunding campaigns through Kickstarter or Go Fund Me where they raised the money they needed for the entire cost of their book production.

For this particular client, I suggested setting up a presale of her book in order to get the money on the front end that she needed to finish the project. She budgeted what she would need to fulfill the book orders once the book was published *and* profit now to get her book finished. She threw together a quick page with a "buy now" link that allowed people to pre-purchase her book before it was completed. Within forty-eight hours she had more than what she needed to complete the production of both of her books.

Your lack of money is a perception. And our perception influences our brain's response. You may not have the dollars in your bank account that you need at this moment, but you have everything you need to add those dollars to your bank account. Instead of believing the message that you don't have enough and therefore cannot afford to do a good job on your book, or even finish your book at all, think about what resources you *do* have available to you. Again, you may have to remind yourself *why this book matters* and who you care about (your target reader).

You're going to need the motivation to put yourself out there to get the dollars you need to finish your book. You're probably going to need some skills you don't have yet. But you know people who do! So "cast your nets" wherever your people hang out, whether that's social media, text, or in-person events you attend like church or school. Ask, "Hey, does anyone know anyone who can brainstorm with me ways to raise money to finish my book?" Or "Hey, is anyone looking for organic soy-based candles? I'm selling some to raise money to publish my book." Pick a hobby and monetize it! It doesn't mean you're going to do this forever or start a new hobby-based business, it just means you believe enough in yourself and your story that you're willing to do what it takes to add the dollars you need to your bank account.

I'm not a huge fan of credit and for many years I haven't held any. So, what I suggest next is presented simply as another possibility that you can use to consider your book production costs. I recently invested in a program to help grow my business beyond the current ceiling it was hitting. I didn't want to use my small savings, so I invited someone to the conversation who geeks out on optimizing credit. This friend found me a credit card with zero percent interest for fifteen months. Now, in my case, the promise of the investment I was making into my business was that I would make back that money quickly if I did what I was told to do in the program. I know I won't need fifteen months to pay back my investment. Still, there's a risk. I *have to do the work* of the program in order to experience the promise of growing my business and income. Yet in this one opportunity, through prayer and conversation with wise and knowledgeable people, I decided to open this line of credit, knowing I'd be charged no interest while I earned the money that I needed to pay off the program.

There are many options out there for this kind of credit. If you're not knowledgeable on this, then do what I did and invite someone who's passionate about optimizing credit, using it for the greatest good and the least amount of financial impact.

But be aware! Selling books takes time and energy. If you're not willing to work hard to sell your books, you won't make the return on your investment to pay off any lines of credit you take to get your book published. Be willing and prepared to do whatever it takes to get your book into the hands of your audience, both for the impact you want to make but also for the income you deserve to make.

Pro Tip:

When you find yourself hearing the message inside your head, "I don't have enough money. I can't afford my dream," pause and begin to brainstorm possibilities for solving that problem. Pull out a sheet of paper or a note on your phone. Ask a friend to hop on a call to brainstorm with you, throw it on the Internet and see what feedback you get. You don't have to rely on the limitations of your own brain and experiences. Lean into that of others and see what ideas come up for you. Maybe it's a fundraiser, maybe it's a presale, maybe it's a line of credit, maybe it's taking on a side job or monetizing a hobby. The money is there and available to you. Will you go get it? Do you believe in your dream? Do you believe in your book? If you don't believe in it, no one else will either. This is an opportunity to show yourself what you are capable of.

Scarcity of Knowledge

This leads really well into another scarcity that many people encounter. It's a scarcity of know-how or knowledge. This is why people hire me. Some people recognize they have a scarcity of knowledge or know-how around the writing or publishing process. But these people didn't stay stuck in that sense of scarcity. Their brains opened up possibility for them because they believe in their message. They watched webinars or joined summits and found me in these places and realized that I *do* have the knowledge and know-how that they *need* to help them cross the finish line with their book. And not just cross the finish line with a crappy book but with a high-quality, professional-looking book that will sell. I *love* that I can offer this skill set and knowledge to people, in the same way that I love that when I lack knowledge or a skillset in some capacity, I can find other people to help me as well.

It's one of my favorite things about humanity—as much as I'd love to be all things to all people, that would exhaust me! I love that each of us is so unique in our desires and passions and skills that we can come together and truly be stronger and better together.

But some people perceive a lack of knowledge as an obstacle to getting it done. They scour the Internet and find tons of contradictory information, spend money for the wrong kind of help, and listen to webinar after webinar after webinar but never take action on what they're learning. They get overwhelmed with all of the information, don't know who to trust, and feel helpless and stuck. All they want to do is get their book into the world and they just don't know how.

It's easy in a scarcity of knowledge to quit, believing that you really just aren't good enough for your story to make it to the world. I can't tell you how many times I've heard an author express feeling dumb for not knowing the process, for trying things that didn't work, wasting time or money, or even investing in a program that scammed them. Their experience reinforces their faulty perception that not knowing what to do equals helplessness and failure.

Well, I'm here to tell you that you *are* good enough and that your book deserves to be in the world and that there are plenty of people with the knowledge you lack to fill in the gaps for you. As I've mentioned before, publishing is a team experience. Every incredible book on the market had a team behind it who brought their own skills, passions, and talents to the project to make it what it is. So, when you feel tempted to be overwhelmed by the process of writing a good book and publishing it, don't allow your brain to get stuck in a freeze state. Don't allow it to remain helpless.

One of my current clients is a very naturally gifted writer, specifically for children. She doesn't have much trouble getting the first draft down but will often look at her first draft and not know how to level it up. Granted, her first draft is usually really good. She likes to meet with me to look at those drafts and bring our minds together to level them up to something that she feels really excited about. Even though she's been in the children's entertainment industry for so long, she knows she needs a team to make her book the best it can be. So even seasoned, prolific people who've been in an industry for a while still invite people to the team to fill in the knowledge gaps. What I appreciate about her is that she knows where to get help, and she's not afraid to ask for it. And she's so humble! This enables her to set her pride aside and focus on the kids she wants to impact through her stories. Even though she has plenty of bragging rights as a well-known voice actress, she doesn't bring pretense to our calls. We've shared many giggles and story epiphanies as she bravely invites me into her imagination poured on a page. *She doesn't stay stuck.* I love this. Her internal messaging isn't one of helplessness but of, "I have the resources I need around me; I just need to ask for them."

Pro Tip:

When you notice a feeling of helplessness in your mind or in your body as you think about everything you don't know, pause and ask yourself *who* do you know? Do you know anyone who's published before? Do you know anyone with connections to someone who's published? Have you watched a webinar with someone you came to trust, who demonstrated they can fill your knowledge gaps? Reach out! You can scour the Internet, there's good information out there... but it's hard to know what's accurate or not and whose information to trust.

For that reason, I created a community called *The Writer's Block* to gather writers and illustrators together and offer monthly expert interviews, group coaching calls, and resources to help save time, money, and energy for authors looking for the knowledge they don't have. So perhaps find a community like that where you trust the people and can get all of your information in one place.

There are some free writing and publishing communities out there as well. However, anyone and everyone joins them and often shares faulty information because anyone can comment or respond without vetting. Some of those "helpers" have published once and believe that their singular experience is *the one way*, the proven path, for everyone. It worked for them, so why not? I'll talk more about that in the next section on a scarcity of self-awareness as we address how important it is to know yourself uniquely so you can discern what will work for you and what won't. While there are some pretty standard elements of the publishing path, there are a number of ways to get there through your own unique wiring. What worked for guru one will be totally different from what works for you. So, find a community with trusted resources where the people giving advice are knowledgeable, trustworthy, experienced in the industry, and have a variety of resources to help every type of person.

Scarcity of Self-Awareness

I stared at my screen. The year was 2020 and I had some unfinished business to deal with.

Two half-finished manuscripts collecting digital dust demanded their turn. A plethora of other books had cut in front of them, taking their moment to shine while these two stood in the corner.

But not quietly. No, they pestered and nagged and whined, "When will you finish me? I want a turn!" Hence #unfinishedbusiness2020.

On impulse, I texted my friend Gary and jokingly accused him of being the culprit behind my writer's block.

"Why aren't you reminding me to write? I have a book to publish, you know!" He didn't even know I was working on a book, y'all. (By the way, I'm always working on a book.)

What I intended as a joke became an actual source of accountability.

Not too long after, my friend Lise turned me onto the Four Tendencies[1]—four different ways that people tend to respond to the expectations placed on themselves and on others.

I took the free quiz and might have cried. "Obliger" was the last thing I wanted to be. It revealed how great I am at honoring the expectations of others, yet struggle to honor my own for myself.

Once I learned this, though, I could set myself up for success. Reaching out to Gary was a way of making my own goal an external expectation. I published *The Abundance of Less* because he expected me to.

Learning about the Four Tendencies by Gretchen Rubin radically changed how I interact with myself *and* how I coach my writing clients. Obligers need me to hold them accountable. Rebels need strong intrinsic motivation. Questioners need me to explain the process and answer any questions, and Upholders need clarity, structure, and patience with the other three tendency types. I brought this awareness to each client and saw them flourish from within their unique wiring.

Sometimes we stare at blank screens because we don't know *ourselves* well enough.

We try to be the "successful" author. We set a goal and then drop everything for the neighbor's need. Or we sit to write and learn the banjo instead (even if you have to buy one to avoid writing. #truestory #rebel) Or we spend all of our writing time researching how to write.

"Know Thyself" is a powerful antidote to writer's block. How do you achieve goals? Study *you* and the words will come.

One of my coaching clients really struggled to get her book written. Every time she sat down to write, she'd have a sudden compulsion to take on a new hobby that never interested her before. We would set goals and she'd promise that *this time* she'd hit them. But on our next call, she could play me a new song on her brand-new banjo but had made no progress on her book. It didn't take me long to wonder if she might be a Four Tendencies Rebel. This time I assigned her to take the free quiz. On our next call, she was in tears. "Marcy, I'm a Rebel! And everything it said about me is so true! I thought I was just a horrible person!"

For her whole life, she'd watched people set goals and hit them with determination, accountability, or some form of grit that she couldn't find in herself. Holding herself up to all of these examples led her to feelings of despair, doubt, and a level of self-loathing. NO! But now she could see that there was a place in the world carved out just for her, and with that knowledge, we could begin to work with *her* in mind, and not everyone else's approach to writing and publishing. With a natural inclination to resist, we had to approach her desire to write a book through the understanding of being a Rebel, which meant focusing on her why, her motivation, her desire to impact, and *not* setting deadlines. A weight was lifted from my sweet client, bigger than just progress on her novel. She inspired me to have all of my coaching clients take the Four Tendencies Quiz before we met so I could tailor my coaching to their uniqueness.

Each of us has unique mental wiring. I encourage you to look into the psychological tool, the Myers-Briggs Type Indicator® (MBTI®), to grow in understanding your wiring. The MBTI looks at your cognitive functions, your own personal mental functioning, and can give you an understanding and language for how *your* mind operates in the world. I'm a bit of an MBTI snob, even going so far as to hire a profiler to help me determine my best fit type (*way* better than an online quiz), become MBTI certified, and join Gary's Changemaker community with a purpose and personality coach focused on personal and professional development through the lens of MBTI. What I've learned is that Myers-Briggs is *way more* than just a set of letters and that most people have *no idea* that it's psychologically based. When it's mentioned in the same sentence as a "What Disney princess are you?" quiz I cringe, and an angel somewhere loses its wings. #SaveTheAngels

Before I encountered tools like MBTI, Enneagram, or CliftonStrengths™ (Strength Finders), I thought I lived in a world full of mirrors. Everyone was revealing to me what I *should* be, and I always fell short. I use an analogy that for most of my life I lived among hammers. They did great work! They got nails in the wall and pulled nails out with that special slotted edge in the back. They were strong, confident, and skilled. I, however, kept trying to bang nails into the wall and getting hurt. I was pretty dinged up and my results were awful—not like the other hammers. Living in their shadow was a constant reminder that something about me was defective. Still, I kept pounding because that's what hammers do.

Then one day I looked in a *real* mirror. And guess what I saw... not a hammer.

I saw a spoon. A dinged-up dented spoon from all the years of trying to get nails in a wall, but a *spoon,* nonetheless. I couldn't believe it! Part of me wanted to cry in grief for all the years I'd lost living like a hammer... and another part wanted to cry in relief—no wonder I wasn't "good enough!" I was running in the wrong lane. I was designed to do dainty things like stir honey into tea, scoop ice cream into delighted mouths, and be the desired token of favorite card games—not pound my head against a metal spike.

The mirror was Myers-Briggs, and my very talented friend held it up for me. In fact, I now joke that he's my Mind Sherpa. Because of his expertise in these tools, he knows my cognitive functions better than I do. I can be mid-sentence and he'll stop to point out what part of my wiring is activated. This is super important because some of our functions are highly developed, and others are more like kids in the backseat of our car... we need to listen to their needs and desires, but we shouldn't let them drive the car! Having a tool like Myers-Briggs has given me the awareness to know whether one of the "kids" is trying to take over or whether I'm operating from the strength of my personal design. It also highlights who I'll need on my team to make up for my own lesser-developed functions. Like the Four Tendencies, knowing my MBTI type has given me eyes to see how *I* operate so that the writing and publishing path I choose for myself is in alignment with how I best operate! No more living like a hammer for me!

While we're all unique, we're unique within some recognizable patterns that enable us to analyze, learn from others, and grow in self-understanding and other awareness. This is crucial in writing and publishing, not to mention in life.

The Enneagram has been useful in showing me how my childhood shaped me, the survival skills I picked up, and which of them still serve me and which don't. It's taught me to recognize my panicky internal response to conflict and my resistance to setting up healthy boundaries (which I do!). It's taught me to measure my energy and budget it well. And it's taught me how to see others as *different* from me.

I had one employer that I was sure regretted hiring me. I always felt called out for not being good enough. He always wanted more of me, which I was sure was a sign that I was the weak link in the chain. One day I was processing this with a dear friend. She said, "Marcy, he sounds like an Enneagram 8. And an 8 interacting with you like that actually sees value and potential in you, and that's why he pushes you so hard." I'm sure my eyes nearly burst from my skull. Everything she was saying made sense. Not too long after, in a playful conversation with my employer, he basically said exactly her words! I had been interacting with that relationship from a place of insufficiency and low worth, simply because I expected him to behave like *me.* As soon as I was given a tool to see *him,* our whole dynamic changed... not because *he* changed, but because my perception of reality shifted from faulty to clear, all because of a tool like the Enneagram.

CliftonStrengths™ is another tool I recommend. This tool looks at your talents and places them on a scale of most developed strength to lesser developed strength. I love the strength's focus. We need reminders that we've been wired for *good* and that we *all* have strengths. This one reminds me that I am strong because I lead with talents like Relator, Empathy, and Connectedness. Those paired with my intuition (MBTI) and my ability to perspective shift (MBTI and Enneagram) give me incredible insight into the inner journey of other humans along with an ability to connect deeply and hang with just about anyone through their messy process. I have a couple of great CliftonStrengths coaches in my life who call me back to a strengths focus when I have personality envy and I love them for it. We're *all* strong in something.

What about you? What are your strengths? Who are your "kids" in the backseat trying to drive your car? How do you show up in times of stress versus times of growth and health? Have you been trying to live like a hammer and feeling pretty dinged up?

I'm so passionate about this topic because of how much it's impacted me. I really did walk this life feeling insignificant and less than at one time. Western culture elevates the opposite of most of my wiring and strengths. This has been true for many of us. Cultural constructs, societal expectations, and family values have all told us we either belong or we don't belong (*cough-cough—a threat to your emotional survival*).

When we don't believe we belong in this era, generation, or world, we will *not* show up in strength for our books. We'll be looking at other writers expecting our journey to look like theirs and failing. We'll look at how others hit their goals (or don't), discipline themselves, or communicate, and always feel we're "not enough."

If you don't know yourself at all, you'll sign up for *every* webinar, summit, or program that promises to get you across the finish line, indiscriminately. When you *know yourself*, you'll choose that path that lines up with who *you* are, and not what worked for some random "hammer." You'll save time, money, and energy because you'll have narrowed down the process that works for you, instead of trying all of them to see which one takes you the furthest. Oh, friend, it actually hurts my heart to see how many people live life blindly—living by default. This way of living is exploited by every marketer who wants your time and money. It's foolish and expensive.

You can try every other tip in this book and *still* make only slow progress if you don't know *yourself*. Not every suggestion in this book will work for everybody! If you come here knowing you need accountability and deadlines, you'll choose the strategies to support that. If you don't, you'll try them all and hope one works.

A scarcity of self-awareness is hardly recognized for what it is. It shows up as exhaustion, frustration, and a lot of sadness. Most people don't realize some personal attention is the solution—but it is!

Pro Tip: Don't use these tools as a way to sabotage your process! If your brain is feeling antsy and avoidant, you may be tempted to hop online and find every quiz you can to learn more about yourself. *Don't.* Knowing yourself is *lifelong* so pace yourself. Start with *one tool.* I have some great resources for you to get you started at the back of the book, so don't worry about that. You can start with an easy, free assessment like the Four Tendencies. You can join a community like the one I'm part of, the Changemaker community, where we meet bi-monthly to dig into who we are and how to make the world a better place. You can start with a book or podcast on the topic. Or you can hire a human (like I did) to interview you and then share your best fit type (and what that means) with you. Do *something* but not *every-*

thing. See more information on the tools (and coaches) I mentioned under "Pro Tips: Quick Reference Guide—Scarcity Blocks."

Scarcity of Inspiration/Creativity

The last scarcity we're going to talk about here is a scarcity of inspiration or creativity. This is almost the definition of writer's block, isn't it? "I'm waiting to feel inspired," you might say. "My muse must be on vacation."

While I admit that it's *really* hard to sit and write when you're just not feeling it, you actually *can* and *should* write, even when you're not feeling it.

A scarcity of inspiration can feel terrifying, especially if your livelihood and income rely on your creativity. This can cause more panic, pulling you into your brainstem. And we all know what happens down there! Panic feeds panic feeds panic, sending us straight into our survival system with even *less* access to our creative brain. So, let's kick the block to the curb so you can write freely and make a reliable (ha!) living from your writing.

Raise your hand if you're a runner.

Fine, raise your hand if you've ever run.

A number of years ago, I decided to train for my first half marathon to raise money for children in Haiti. These weren't just any children; these were children that were closely connected to friends of mine who were personally starting an orphanage and a couple of schools. I had the deep honor of going to Haiti with them and photographing the kiddos for their sponsorship cards (among other activities). Don't be fooled... my love for orphans is one of the few things that would convince my body to *run*.

I trained with my friends, who were also coaches, and beat my body into shape. Well, it more beat *me* into shape, but I did it. I kept showing up. I remember the first day of the first training when I was supposed to run a quarter mile. I remembered back to being in elementary school and having to lap our schoolyard, grabbing a popsicle stick every time we passed the teacher to remember how many laps we'd completed. I always came in last at around twelve minutes a mile. That number stayed with me as a disgrace. I said this to my coach friend. "Ericlee, I think I run about a twelve-minute mile... that's pretty bad, right? Will I ever get faster?" He smiled.

"That's actually pretty good..." (I mean, all things considered). My memory fooled me into thinking my body still ran twelve-minute miles. I knew I'd come in last, I just thought I'd do it faster. That first day of training, I couldn't even run for a whole quarter mile. And I certainly wasn't pacing at a twelve-minute mile. In fact, I haven't seen a twelve-minute mile since I was ten years old.

But as I showed up each day and trained, my body was able to run further and further. I remember our six-mile training day. We were running in a not-great part of town and most of our team didn't show up. The only ones who came were actual twelve-minute milers and I knew I'd be alone in the shady part of town, miles from my car or a friend should I need an escape. And that's exactly how it started... my teammates were off, and I was the slow but steady tortoise. I felt some anxiety the further I got from my car and teammates. I heard my coach's voice in my head, "Running is about your mindset. Your body can *always* do more than you *think* it can." I decided to test him. I had some motivation... outrun any bad guys. I began to pace myself with the street blocks... run one, walk one, run one, walk one. Once I had a good rhythm, I decided to push myself: run two, walk one. Before I knew it, I'd caught up to my teammates! (One of them had a cramp so they'd slowed down, but you can still imagine my relief and sense of accomplishment!)

When I got to the end of my six miles, most of the rest of the team had already finished and gone home, but I'd *done it.* I'd proven to myself that my body could do more than my mind believed it could. I gave my whole person an experience with overcoming a mindset belief. I was ecstatic. I shifted my belief from, "I'm going to be last and alone in a scary part of town which makes me either about to die or a big loser," to, "Wow! Look at me go! All that training is paying off! My body is showing up for me and I'm so proud of myself. I didn't know I had it in me!" My brain had been hyper-vigilant about the risks in front of me, but instead of choosing my survival brain (I would have "flighted" right back to my car and into my bed at home), I gave it an experience with meeting a challenge face on and *winning*.

This is what we need to do with our writing.

It takes training... putting your butt in a seat and doing the work, even when you don't feel like it. It takes putting yourself in places where your creativity tank can be *filled* so it's not empty when it's time for you to *pour*.

On race day, the air was filled with anticipation. Our training runs leading up had already had us over the thirteen-mile mark, so I *knew* I could do it. But how last would I be doing it? (Also, can we talk about marathon training that takes you over your race mileage? Where is the medal and food at the end of that training?! It was always annoying to me that I'd basically already run the half-marathon but without all the fanfare).

My coach's wife, a good friend of mine, pulled me aside so we could warm up. We stretched, as I expected. And then she said, "Okay, let's run a mile."

What?

Why in the world would I add a mile to my already really long run? No, thanks.

She reminded me that the first mile is always the worst. The lactic acid, the cold muscles, the body that thought it would be sleeping on this fine Sunday morning... makes the first mile one of burning legs and lungs. "So why not get that mile out of the way so we can start the race ready to go?"

Dang. She had a point. Which was a little irritating because I was still psychologically unprepared to run 14.3 miles that day, but I couldn't resist her logic. So, we ran our one mile—and she was right! The start of the race felt amazing (not to be confused with the end of the race when I felt like a zombie, limp-running across the finish line with both hips and a knee out of place. But I did it!)

This. Is. Writing.

When you sit down to write and you feel uninspired, guess what? You've got to move the "lactic acid," warm up the muscles, and tell your body and brain that this is *exactly* what you do on a fine Monday afternoon. The first "mile" of writing can suck. It can burn. It can take your breath away. It can make you feel like quitting. You can fall into the trap of believing that the *whole* writing day is going to feel like that first "mile." Who wants that torture?

But just like a long run, your brain needs you to get the first "mile" out of the way so you can have an amazing writing time. You have to support the transition from whatever you *were* doing to this incredible place of creativity, and you can do that by writing through the pain.

Faulkner is quoted as saying, "I only write when inspiration strikes. Fortunately, it strikes at nine every morning." Faulkner knew the power of showing up. He didn't *wait* for inspiration; he had a standing appointment with it.

I also think of it this way. No one expects their garden to produce a harvest without clearing the stones, weeds, and nurturing the soil. Planting a garden means clearing a space. It means sitting in the dirt and pulling out everything that won't support the growth of your vegetable. If you sit around waiting for the land to make space for your garden, you'll be waiting and without a garden for your whole life. You have to show up to the plot of land and create the space for growth.

This is like the first "mile" of a run. Your brain may not feel inspired with all the weeds and surface gunk covering the good nutritious soil beneath. You have to uproot the weeds and clear the surface stuff to get to the nutrients. This is what the first "mile" of writing is like—putting weedy words on a page to clear the surface of your brain so you can get to the good stuff.

Or think of it this way. You know how you have to burn the first few pancakes before they start cooking perfectly? Sometimes, your brain needs to "burn some pancakes" before it starts producing the best stuff. It's part of the process.

Have you ever gotten into a good writing groove? Like, something clicked as you were writing and suddenly you were *in the flow*, unstoppable, and putting down words you actually *liked*. It's an amazing feeling. It's like the runner's high, but better because you're not running, you're *creating*. The wind is blowing your hair, the angels are singing, and you can see The NY Times Best Seller list just around the corner.

You got to that moment because you *started*, not because your muse came home from Fiji.

A scarcity of inspiration is really a scarcity of *starting*.

Put the weedy, junky words on a page, not because they're good or going to be part of your published work, but because they're *in the way*. And the only way to get them out of the way is to let them out. You can burn the page, delete the words, whatever; it doesn't matter. What matters is you did the hard work so *now* you can benefit from the harvest.

It's not about a muse or a feeling of inspiration, it's about a decision. You can "weed" your creativity by writing about how you don't feel inspired to write, but you're doing it anyway, so here are my words while I write my first "mile" and get my brain to agree that we're going to write this book come fire or hail or another round of Covid. Before you know it, you'll be writing something brilliant.

A scarcity of inspiration *used* to leave you feeling panicky and unmotivated. But now that you have some tools and strategies for treating this form of writer's block, you don't have to stay stuck anymore. When your brain is tempted to freeze in the helpless feeling of a blank screen and no inspiration, re-read this chapter and get to it. Your brain (and readers) will thank you.

Pro Tip: Sometimes you can sit and write through the first "mile" and still just feel so empty. This is an indicator that your art tank is empty. Just like runners make sure they've given their body the sources of energy it needs before a big run (the large pasta meal the day before), you need to give your brain the creative sources of energy it needs. You can't expect your creativity tank to pour endlessly without being refilled periodically. How you fill your creative tank will be as unique as you are!

So, let's address the weary soul. Your creativity (even the creativity of putting a real story to paper) is like a car. You want it to give and give... take you all the places and carry all your friends, but it can only do that with gas in the tank.

Years ago, I sat in a workshop led by the talented and prolific writer of multiple genres, Laurie Halse Anderson. I was a new writer waiting for inspiration to strike. She stressed the importance of art dates to keep our relationship with our creativity strong. Just like time and distance from a loved one may lead to feelings of disconnection, so time and distance from our creativity will feel the same. The more time between art "touches," the harder it is to get back to our own creativity. We need to nurture this relationship like we would with anyone we love. Time, attention, affection, and care will feed your creative soul to a point of overflowing.

Make a list of the different ways other forms of art fill your soul. Then take regular art dates to nourish your creative energy. Here are some ideas:

- Go to an art gallery or museum and take in the artwork.
- Attend a concert and soak up the music.
- Scroll Pinterest and savor all of your favorite images or ideas.
- Go for a nature walk or run and notice the natural beauty of creation.
- Take a bath while listening to your favorite playlist.
- Put your hands in clay and play (with no agenda for the end product).
- Enjoy a ballet or live stage performance of some kind.
- Take a class in a form of art that makes you happy.
- Dance like no one is watching (or watch someone else dance).
- Drive around your city and notice the street art or murals. Cities like New York City and London are known for their graffiti as *art.* Take notice of what's in *your* own city.
- Take a walk in your downtown and appreciate the architecture. What makes it unique from other places?
- Laugh with a comedian.
- Marvel at a magician.
- Watch pour-painting art videos on YouTube.
- Read a novel.
- Attend a paint night (yes, you're producing but being told what to do. This can get you in touch with your creative energy without putting it in the position of creating something original).

Whatever gives your art tank *life* and *energy* to give to your page, go do it.

This list is by no means complete, but hopefully gives you an idea of how varied your art dates can be. My favorite art date involves a rooftop and an ocean. I love to sit at my favorite inn with the expanse of the sea before me, the wildlife playing in the waves, and the white noise of people enjoying the time and place on the earth. With a slight breeze, the fire pit lit, and a panorama of beauty, I can write forever. Art is as much in nature as it is in a museum or on a stage or in a book. Find the art that fills your tank and *receive*.

CHAPTER SIXTEEN

scarcity blocks

GRAB THE WRENCH

GRAB THE WRENCH

You've done a lot of reading. I gave you a *ton* beneath the hood. Now it's time to take action. Don't just take in good ideas and do nothing with them. Get going! If you're stuck on where to start, go on an art date! If your creative tank is indicating full, then write through that first "mile." Or if you're overwhelmed with what you don't know, take one of the assessments or hire some time with a coach to talk you through your unique wiring and the right author journey for *you*. (See my recommended coaches at the back of the book).

Scarcity blocks are only your *sense* of lack related to your resources of time, money, and know-how, as well as your creative energy and self-awareness. Staying in a perception of lack will prevent you from feeling equipped or motivated to move forward, blocking your work. The good news is—you can change your perception! Refer to any number of the analogies in this section to help you reframe your perception from one of helpless scarcity to an achievable abundance of possibility!

When you're staring at a blinky cursor and have no idea how to move it—fill your tank! Close the computer, set down the pen, and give yourself an art date—fill yourself so that you have a well to pull from when it's time to pour.

Don't wait until you're out of gas, feeling like a failure. Treat your tank regularly.

CHAPTER SEVENTEEN

scarcity blocks

BACK ON THE ROAD

GET BACK ON THE ROAD

Scarcity of inspiration or creativity can be debilitating, but as you know now, it doesn't have to be. It's a decision to show up for inspiration instead of waiting for it to show up for you. Don't be mastered by some mystical muse. Take the reins of your author journey. You have everything you need for the *next step*.

And don't stay in learning mode—get writing! Like, right now. Put this book down and go do something to move your book forward. I'll still be here when you get back.

> *"Writer's block is a misnomer and can be compared with turning off a faucet. Like the ability to write, faucets can develop problems when they're seldom used. You get all this rust in the pipes. When you turn on the faucet, a lot of rust comes out."*
>
> *—SUSAN NEVILLE*

attentional blocks

"A writer is somebody for whom writing is more difficult than it is for other people."

—Thomas Mann

CHAPTER EIGHTEEN

attentional blocks

THE GEEK OUT

Irony of all ironies, I keep getting distracted as I try to sit and work on this section today. We're here to talk about Attentional Blocks, when our focus and attention are easily drawn away from our creativity due to personal life challenges, capacity, and neurology.

Or in my case today, ongoing distraction.

My distractions are both internal and external.

Many of us easily recognize external distractions. I'm a single mama homeschooling my kids while running my business from home. Two-thirds of that sentence wasn't my first choice but here I am. My kids are older now so there's a level of independence they have in their schooling, but there are plenty of meetings to attend, papers to file or email, screenshots to grab, and schoolwork to help with. Writing a book while homeschooling, or even parenting at all, is an uphill battle.

The other day I told my family that I was going to my room to work on my book.

Everyone followed me.

First my sister. Then my daughter. Then my son, who felt left out upon entering and seeing everyone hanging out. None of our kitties or pups were to be outdone by these humans, so they joined us too. All five of them. Right after I said, "Ciao, everyone, I'm off to write."

Yes, of course, I can lock my door. I can place the door hanger I made to communicate when I'm unavailable. I could leave the house. Or yell at them to leave me alone.

But these days with my kids wanting to hang out on my bed are numbered and I savor them... often at the expense of my own book. Cohabitating with other living creatures is distracting. If it's not the kids, it's a cat trying to lie on my keyboard while I type. Or a puppy who wants outside. Yes, I basically live in the circus.

Other distractions are internal. The reason I'm a newly single mama is full of tragedy and recovery, major life adjustments, the burial of dreams, and the birth of new ones. Sadness and relief dance throughout my days, less as each one passes, but a constant, none-theless. When the imposter shows up, she's as distracting as a clown at a kid's party—but only in my head. Some days I have my internal fly swatter constantly batting away the messages flying at my face. Today is one of those days.

Keeping our attention on the things that matter is an act of a sheer will, and that's not just a saying!

THE GEEK OUT

Let's dive into your brain and attention.

In a world *saturated* with information coming at you from every direction, your brain has the incredibly high-paced, detail-oriented, risk-riddled job of remaining constantly alert and vigilant, selecting what information gets your notice and what doesn't, directing that information, and filtering that information. I'm exhausted thinking about it.

My friend Dillon Barr, an author in his own right, regularly teaches strategies for holding and directing attention. One of his favorite resources for this is Gurdjieff, an Armenian philosopher and mystic, who took a deep *attentive* look at how we hold attention.

Gurdjieff[1] suggests three "Qualities of Attention" which I find fascinating.

The first quality is *mechanical* attention, or a "floating" attention. This is a free-floating undirected attention which simply hops from interest to interest with no real plan or intention. It has no roots or anchor, just carries us along any current that comes our way. We don't usually remember what caught our mechanical attention, it just flits by. This is attention with no focus or particular subject, low-quality, neutral, and passive. I imagine a blossom that has fallen from its tree simply floating on the wind, falling where it falls, lifting when the wind is strong enough. We spend a lot of time here!

The second quality is *emotional* attention, in which something catches our notice and holds it with a kind of riveting fascination. This might occur when we read a book, watch a show or movie, come upon an emergency situation or scene... anything that catches our otherwise floating attention and draws it in, sometimes to the degree that we become oblivious to anything else going on around us. While this quality of attention has a direction, it isn't based on one's will, but on a fascination that caught the passing attention. I imagine this quality is a little like a cat.

My experience with cats is that they act disinterested most of the day but can easily become engrossed in something that catches their eye. For one of my cats, Popcorn, that could be the lid to a squeeze apple sauce or a hair tie. (She loves taking our rubber bands and leaving them in water dishes). Our other cat, Cinder, seems to suddenly notice her tail each night around 7 p.m. It becomes the object of her obsession for the next ten minutes as she spins and spins. Emotional attention finds a point of fascination (like a car accident) and focuses there temporarily, without any predetermination or will.

The third quality is *directed* attention. This is the attention you predecide to give. Before the focal point of your attention is even present, you've made a decision to concentrate on it. Do you see the importance of language? This is where the largest *concentration* of your *attention* is purposeful, intentional, and conscious. It requires strenuous effort as it fights the pull of the competing mechanical and emotional attentions. We spend the least amount of time in directed attention, and yet it can lead to some of our most profound experiences and core memories. It requires *presence* and *intentionality*.

Are you trying to write your book with mechanical or emotional attention?

Imagine entering a noisy concert hall to see your favorite band. As you walk up to the ticket taker, people and sounds surround you... but you're all eyes for that ticket taker. Once you've displayed your ticket, you have to find your seat. You pass the merch tables, the snack shacks, the posters for next week's concert, and the bathrooms... well, maybe not the bathrooms. But you pass everything else with a fixation that's almost unbreakable. You're focused on finding the D door which holds your D52 seat. Suddenly you hear your name called and you turn to see your best friend approaching. With hundreds of people talking and laughing all around you, your brain picked out the sound of your name from the voice of your best friend. You hug and walk into the D door together. You walk down a set of shallow stairs until you find your aisle, scooting into your number and taking a seat.

"Our brain is constantly bombarded with stimuli: the senses of sight, hearing, smell, and touch transmit millions of bits of information per second."[2] That's incredible! And it has to make decisions about those bits of information nearly as fast as they come in.

Imagine a world in which you go to that same noisy concert hall, but *everything* stands out to you. The colors, the smells, the visuals, the sounds... every single word within your hearing, you hear it, *really* hear it. The sensory overload would probably have you on the floor in the fetal position.

It's easy to take our brains for granted. So, let's pause for a second and appreciate the incredible amount of work it does to keep you alive and thriving. Thank you, Brain, for keeping me from the fetal position on the concert hall floor.

Now, how does your brain know what to bring to your attention and what not to? You get to decide. You can either train your brain or be ruled by it. Remember the Reticular Activating System, RAS, from Mental Blocks? Here it is again. The things we choose to think about will continually be highlighted for us. The things that we value (finding our concert seat) will guide what our brain chooses to discard, file away, or bring to your attention.

I love this comment by William James, the founding father of American psychology, in his 1890 book, *The Principles of Psychology.*

He says,

> Millions of items of the outward order are present to my senses which never properly enter into my experience. Why? Because they have no interest for me. *My experience is what I agree to attend to.* Only those items which I notice shape my mind. (emphasis mine)

This is attention. This is sheer will.

You can shape it or be controlled by it. Notice how he says, "*...what I agree to attend to.*" Deep in your brain is a process through which your focus and attention are *decided.* In those snap moments, you make mostly subconscious decisions about what will hold your interest and what won't. But you can also predetermine what will get your attention.

Now imagine sitting in your seat in the concert hall. Look around: what do you see? Now close your eyes and listen. There are voices talking all around you, each an individual waiting for the same concert to begin. Your best friend is talking, tune in. Now, tune out your best friend's voice and choose to pick up the conversation of a couple sitting a few seats away. Now take a deep breath. What do you notice?

This is intentional attention. When you choose to be present and attuned, you can orient your brain's processing to focus on what you want to notice. Most of the time, though, we just subject ourselves to the process without much *presence*.

Some of us have a deficit of attention. We may not *say* it that way. "I have a lack of attention right now, so I can't write." But we *will* say things like, "I can't focus," "My brain is scattered," or, "What was I just doing? I can't remember." We live by default, constantly reacting to all of the information coming at us, handing over the power to our incredible but still limited brain. Without your direction, your brain does its best based on a number of indicators, but it can definitely mess up!

Imagine being in the concert hall again. Your best friend is talking and you're doing your best to pay attention. But suddenly you hear the word "taco" a few rows over and your ears perk up. Immediately it's as if you're in the middle of their conversation. They're talking about the new taco stand in town and you've been wondering if it's any good. They seem to think it was decent—

"Hey, are you listening?" your best friend says, bringing you back to the person beside you. Whoops! You allowed your brain to make a decision about where to direct your focus (because who wouldn't be distracted by tacos?) and missed the more important things, or *person,* right in front of you.

CHAPTER NINETEEN

attentional blocks

THE CHECK ENGINE LIGHT

ENGINE CHECK

Attentional blocks can show up because of personal life challenges like divorce, caregiving, parenting, sudden (or even slow) death of a loved one, financial stressors, loss of a job, or any life change or challenge. It can also show up through disorders like Attention Deficit (Hyperactivity) Disorders (I mean, it's *in the name*). All of these hijack our typical thought processes and tax our energy. They cause us to live in an info-overload that is emotional, physical, mental, and spiritual. Life challenges and disorders make our typical automated processing even more difficult, as the brain is either struggling to wrap around the life change or doesn't have the neurotypical functioning to process information as others do.

Let's check in and see how these might manifest in our everyday life.

Have you ever sat down at your computer and realized you'd been staring at your screen for a solid five minutes while you daydreamed about what you wanted for dinner or replayed a conversation you had earlier in the week? No? Just me?

Even in the last twenty minutes of working on this chapter, I've found myself on Wish (I almost never shop on Wish), going through the photos on my phone, taking yet *another* adorable picture of my dog, and basically anything but writing this chapter.

Have you ever looked up from your device and thought, "How in the world did I get here and how long have I been so distracted?" Oh, man.

Here are other "symptoms" that might get your Attentional check engine light all lit up:

1. Wandering mind and daydreaming.
2. Not finishing anything you start (with multiple unfinished tasks everywhere).
3. Saying "yes" to any request.
4. Finding your attention easily pulled in every direction ("Squirrel!").
5. Finding yourself down a rabbit hole you had no intention of being in.
6. Difficulty following directions.
7. Forgetfulness (What did I come into this room for?).
8. Trouble keeping track of personal items (like keys, glasses, wallet, water bottle, etc.).
9. Short attention span.
10. Trouble multi-tasking.
11. Missing important details.
12. Task-hopping.

All of these attentional symptoms can occur with too little sleep, poor nutrition, illness, or overwhelm. A friend recovering from an illness texted today and said, "Brain fog is real and it's embarrassing. Twice today I couldn't remember what to do with the work report that came in, even though I regularly review them and *have for the last four years.*" Her brain and body are focused on healing physically, not reviewing work reports.

Between the impact of our life challenges, our neurology, and our health, concentrating on writing your book can be hard! It's no wonder you sometimes just stare at your page and zone out.

So, let's get beneath the hood and see what's *really* going on when we find ourselves distracted.

CHAPTER TWENTY

attentional blocks

BENEATH THE HOOD

BENEATH THE HOOD

Attentional blocks can leave us feeling discouraged and dumb. "Why can't I just follow through? Why can't I stop losing things? How am I busy all day but never get anything done?" Maybe you've caught yourself in this cycle of questions. Feeling scattered while trying to be productive is frustrating.

It's easy to assign meaning to the experience of distraction. "I'm getting old," or, "I think I might have ADD," or, "I'm so stupid, why can't I remember important details?!" Grab these messages when you hear them! Make a conscious effort to *notice* the messages that immediately follow an experience with scarce attention and challenge them.

"Yes, maybe I'm aging (we all are) but I intend to be an active, healthy, young aging person. That's not what's impacting my ability to focus. Am I getting enough sleep? Dealing with extra stress? My body is talking to me; what can I do to support my body?"

"I *might* have ADD (it's worth looking into) and if I do, learning that will help me know how to accommodate life expectations through that lens and with appropriate medication. But I also might not... are there other possible factors? Let me reflect on the last day or two and notice what might be pulling at my attention."

"I feel tempted to think badly of myself for missing important details. But I'm not stupid, I'm human. I have a lot going on right now. I need to give myself grace. This is a sign that my brain needs a break. What can I do to help?"

Flip the script. This is not only *honest*, but it supports your brain, redirects your RAS, and brings focused attention instead of mechanical attention.

There are so many things in life vying for your attention! We have more access to information in one minute than ever before in history. Some of that information sits there waiting for us to find it... and other information is nearly knocking down our doors to get access to our minds, our hearts, and our wallets.

> *It wouldn't be an exaggeration to say that smartphone notifications impact your brain on a daily basis. 'It sends our brain into overdrive, triggering anxiety and stress, and at the very least, hyper-vigilance, which is meant to protect ourselves from predators, not the phone,' Dr. Sanam Hafeez, PsyD, a licensed psychologist and professor at Columbia University in New York City, tells Bustle. 'The alerts from phones or even the anticipation of them, shuts off the prefrontal cortex that regulates higher-level cognitive functions, and instead, forces the brain to send emergency signals to the body.'*[1]

The constant influx of communication has our brains in overdrive, pulling them away from our critical thinking and into a stress state.

The trouble is that our brain also experiences these notifications as a reward! The release of dopamine with each new ding reinforces to our brain the importance of the distraction. It's kind of like a trauma bond—our body experiences stress, then reward, then stress, then reward, eventually creating a dysfunctional relationship between the two.

I can't stand unaddressed notifications on my phone. It's like an open loop that I feel compelled to close (Thanks a lot, dopamine). It's distracting. When I realized how quickly I *reacted* to that little notification number on my phone, I had to make some changes. I noticed that when I woke up in the morning, I grabbed my phone and the first thing I saw was my email notifications. With a foggy morning brain, I'd quickly scan the emails. Any of them that required a response got one. Instead of waking up slowly and peacefully, I kept forcing myself to wake up to the noise of a very busy email inbox. And because I wasn't fully awake, I'd miss important details, forget I ever read an email (and therefore not respond), or feel anxious until I could complete a task for a client. It was awful.

It finally occurred to me one day to remove the email app from my phone. Yep. The only way I see email now is when I choose to log in through my computer. I set aside time in my calendar to address my email once or twice a day and that's it. The weight that has been lifted from my shoulders with this one small change is profound. In fact, it's motivated me to make other changes just like it.

The symptoms we experience with the check engine light are indicators of something deeper going on. Our brain is being forced away from autopilot, needs some direction, is overwhelmed with additional information to process (life challenges or our socials blowing up), a legitimate need to focus on another function (healing), or an actual disorder.

Yet we rarely stop to notice *why* we keep getting distracted or can't seem to focus. Not only are we not challenging the messages that come with those distractions, but we're not addressing the root issues: we need to discipline our minds or address the overwhelm.

So, let's grab the wrench and get to business.

CHAPTER TWENTY-ONE

attentional blocks

GRAB THE WRENCH

GRAB THE WRENCH

WHAT CAN we do to bring our attention back to our book?

I won't lie, some days it's *a lot* of work. I'm living one of them. I've been constantly battling to keep my thoughts *here.* As I bring my attention to what's distracting me, I address it. Do the notifications popping up on my phone or screen keep getting my "click" and taking me down a rabbit hole? Then I turn on my Do Not Disturb (DND) and get back to work. It might take me a few rabbit holes before I realize what's happening, but as soon as I do, I address it. It's no wonder we say to "pay" attention. There's a cost! But the cost is worth it.

Because *you* matter. You matter more than the latest Instagram notification or TikTok live or sale at Michaels. YOU are where I want to direct my attention, and so I'm doing the hard work of pulling my energy back your way.

Sometimes it feels like I'm wearing a resistance band. My gym coach has us put a resistance band around our hips, with it tethered to the wall behind us. Then we're supposed to squat jump away from the wall. I do the hard work but hardly cover any distance before I'm pulled back to where I started, only to begin again. Over and over. Sometimes sitting to write and stay focused feels just like a resistance band pulling me back against the wall, away from my writing. But just like those jump squats, the more you practice pulling your attention back and *choosing* to focus, the more brain "muscle" you develop. You are training your brain on the things that matter to you.

And you matter to me.

Gurdjieff[1] talks about training our attention. Through a variety of practices, much like the resistance band, we can train our minds to spend more time in *directed* attention. This is a wonderful option to consider if you begin to notice how little time you spend there. The brain is *incredible.* It is always changing, adjusting, and creating new pathways. We call this plasticity. As we experience new things, our brain rewires and creates connections in response. This is learning... information that gets taken in and applied. If we aren't learning, our brain isn't changing or growing. And a brain that doesn't change or grow becomes stagnant and lazy.

My friend Dillon, who I mentioned earlier, often talks about divided or split attention. There's a *lot* that can be said on this topic and I risk oversimplifying it by not taking you deep into the divided attention weeds, but I want to give you enough to know these concepts exist and send you off to do any research that you think will support your own author journey. Divided attention is the idea that if you can ground an aspect of your attention in *one* place, you can give more attention to *a different* place. This is largely an external anchoring and an internal "paying attention to." Dillon's demonstration of this practice was to hold a pen and roll it between his fingers while he listens to someone. He finds that the grounding activity of giving his body an assigned sensory activity frees his mind to maintain presence and attunement more easily.

I experienced this as a child (um, and adult). As a young student, I learned that if I doodled while I listened, I heard everything the teacher said. Teachers didn't love what appeared to be distractibility during their lectures. They also didn't love when you covered your hand in glue, let it dry, and peeled it off while they were talking. They made me stop and look at them. The problem was that as soon as my hands weren't assigned an activity, my brain wandered, and I daydreamed through the whole lecture. Little Marcy was already practicing this deep concept of divided attention, not to be philosophical or ahead of her time, but because this was the greatest support to her learning. (If you're an educator, I *highly* recommend you spend some time looking into this concept and making space for it/encouraging it in your classroom). I've noticed more commercialized fidget toys hit the market to encourage this, like fidget spinners and pop its. There's definitely more awareness around this now and I'm grateful.

Even now, if I know I have a long meeting I'll bring a coloring book and colored pencils. For many years I attended an hours-long dinner and presentation. It didn't require much of me other than to dress nice and clap for all the people. The tables were long, and the dining hall made conversation difficult. I remember getting some side eyes the first time I colored the night away. But the next year, someone else brought theirs too. And the year after that also. We have a strange social construct that if I'm not staring at you during your long lecture, I'm not paying attention. Sometimes that's true! But sometimes it's *how* I pay attention. Other times I can choose to pull against the resistance band and keep directing my attention back because that communicates care to the person speaking.

Try it out! Put a tennis ball under your foot while you write. Try grounding yourself in a point of sensory attention and see if it gives your mind the freedom to focus on your book. You may find that this is more distracting than helpful—great! Now you know. Not every tool will work for everyone. This is part of the Know Thyself journey... find what works and toss what doesn't.

There are a number of other things I do to keep my focus where I *want* it, pull as it might toward the plethora of distractions.

Pro Tip: I usually set my DND before I start writing, but sometimes I forget. As soon as I remember, I turn it on. Then there's way less getting through the barrier to disrupt me. You can also just turn off the wi-fi or data. That'll do it too!

If it's my home life interrupting me, I put a door hanger on the door. If that doesn't work, I *lock* the door. If *that* doesn't work, I leave the house. I've trained my family to recognize the door hanger and respect it. But every now and then they need a reminder. OR their interruption reminds me I didn't hang it. This is also a work in boundary setting.

Bonus Pro Tip: I used to really struggle with boundaries. Saying "no" or "later" is really hard for me. The possibility that my kids will think I value my work over *them* is enough to get me to close my computer and orbit their planets. This is where boundaries and communication are so helpful! My kids *know* that I'm one hundred percent for them. They also know that my business feeds us. And that it feeds me. Not with food, but my actual soul. I *love* helping authors develop their stories, heal from them, and get them into the world. I'm a champion for my kids to do the same (Hence why I'm currently sitting in the mall across from Payless while my daughter takes two acting classes. Yes, I rearranged the mall's sitting furniture to suit my business needs. Yes, I put it back when I'm done). I want my kids to know their dreams matter by showing them what *dreams that matter* look like! Not at their expense but *for* their expense. This means I ask them to honor my writing hours, and then I commit to honoring my time with them.

So, bring and keep your attention on your writing by reducing and removing distractions. You can do this digitally and personally.

Bonus Pro Tip: If you have to work in a busy place, like a cafe or, ahem, a mall... bring headphones. I usually forget mine and it's inevitable that a stranger will approach me like we're besties, even though I've rearranged the furniture, have my computer on my lap, and look like a serious, professional writer. I told my friend that I should make a shirt, "Writer at work. Do NOT talk or you'll get written in... and it won't be good." But my friend thought a better idea was to wear headphones. He's probably right. He also suggested that I don't look up from the computer, even when the sweetest woman passes by and says, "Oh! Your hair is so pretty! I love all the colors." (How do you not look up and bless that angel for her kindness? Psh.) So, if your writing occurs in a busy place, bring headphones... and maybe my shirt idea.

Bonus Pro Tip: If you find you need to research information in order to move forward, you can do a couple of things. Sometimes I leave a note to myself like "Add statistic/quote/fact here" and keep writing. If the information I need to find impacts my ability to move forward, then I set a timer for ten or fifteen minutes and I research my heart out. Knowing the clock is ticking keeps me focused on finding the information I need. Otherwise, I end up watching an hour documentary on World War I or have read a dissertation on the importance of dirt before I remember that I'm supposed to be writing my book.

Bonus Pro Tip: When you stop writing for the day, stop in a place where you know EXACTLY what's coming next. Most authors write until they don't know what to say and call it a day. The next day... you're staring at a cursor. Leave yourself a gift for the next writing session and stop while it's going well! This will give a focal point for your attention and retain it sooner and longer.

Bonus Pro Tip: Trick your brain into focusing! Decide to free write about something you like (aka a current interest) and just write something small about it. It doesn't have to be amazing or anything you'll use, just bring your attention to something you enjoy and write! This will get your brain to join you in the writing experience. Once you're locked in, segue to writing your book.

Bonus Pro Tip: If you get bit by the "New Idea Syndrome" it's time to pull out a sheet of paper and take notes. Those little buggers want to derail and distract you with every shiny new idea. Give your brain the satisfaction of writing it down for safekeeping (who knows, maybe it's your next bestseller?) But *keep writing*.

CHAPTER TWENTY-TWO

attentional blocks

BACK ON THE ROAD

GET BACK ON THE ROAD

Wow! Did you struggle to stay focused in this section? I did! Not because it wasn't amazing (ha!) but because it's hard work. *Paying* attention takes effort. But just like the resistance band gave me incredible quads and glutes, directing your attention will strengthen your focus, improving your overall health.

If you find yourself derailed from writing because of an attentional scarcity, you now have a number of tips to get back on the road. There are practical tips, like turning off your sound and notifications, wearing homemade shirts (and headphones) to the mall, or setting clear boundaries around your writing time. And there's some internal personal development work you can do by training your brain and practicing presence.

Just like most blocks, bringing your awareness to what's getting in your way and *choosing* to kick that block to the curb is crucial. Writing is not a passive project. It takes *all* of you. Most writers don't realize this when they get started. I've met a number of people who thought they'd sail through their retired years writing best-selling books that would set them up to finish life on cruise ships. Writing is a transformational experience in nearly every possible way. Take this section, for example. If you address your attentional blocks so you can finish your book... think of how different your *whole life* will be as a result? The ways we adjust to commit to the promise we made ourselves that we would publish this book are life-changing. Not to mention the incredible power of keeping your promises. There's almost nothing greater you can give yourself.

procedural blocks

"Don't stop because you've hit a block. Finish the page, even if you write nothing but your own name. The block will break if you don't give in to it. Remember, writing is a physical habit as well as whatever you want to think it is—calling, avocation, talent, genius, art."

—Isabelle Holland

CHAPTER TWENTY-THREE

procedural blocks

THE GEEK OUT

This is one of my favorite blocks to talk about. While there are still self-messages, brain training, and underlying causes of procedural blocks, I find it to be the easiest of the blocks to resolve. This is the section where you get to say, "Marcy. Listen. I've got all the internal work done. I'm fearless and self-adjusted. My focus is like a laser beam. *I just need to know what to do.*" Yay! Then you're in the right section.

Procedural Blocks are usually caused by our habits, routines, systems, and workflow. They are a matter of discipline, adjustments to our process, and helping our brain create important associations. (I told you the brain will join us in every chapter!)

So, let's dive in!

THE GEEK OUT

The brain is like a muscle. It's *not* technically a muscle, but many of the ways that we work to grow, strengthen, or train a muscle, we can do with our brain as well. As we've covered in other sections, our brain loves autopilot and patterns. The more it can connect elements of life together, the more it can set to cruise control and happily focus on the more pressing needs. At this point in my writing and publishing career, my brain is able to set most of the publishing process on autopilot. I could probably publish a book in my sleep. (I've seen some sleepwalkers who probably *could* publish a book in their sleep! HA!)

There are other things in life that derail me every day. Homeschooling is one of them. I have no idea what I'm doing. I've partnered with a charter school, I have a liaison, funding, and a list of standards for each of the core subjects. But while I've been a student for a *lot* of years, I'm not an educator. This is a place where I can easily fall into a place of helplessness and *freeze.* In fact, I had a mini sob-fest today over math. I feel as lost and helpless with homeschooling as many of my clients feel when we start working together.

I recently met with an author who hired my *Done-With-You* service. In this experience, my authors get coaching calls and a checklist of every step they'll take from draft to publish (and a bit beyond). There are links to tutorial videos, articles, and all of the platforms they'll need in order to successfully publish a high-quality book. They get referrals to cover designers and formatters and anyone else they might need. It's an opportunity to learn to "fish" especially if they have multiple books. This particular author really wanted to learn for herself. She's in her seventies, active, and intelligent. She also recently lost her husband to Covid. Her blocks are a combination of scarcity (know-how), attentional (major life change with her husband's death), and procedural (technology-overwhelmed). That's partly what our coaching calls are for!

However, on today's call, she came to the conclusion that she'd like my *Done-For-You* help to get her book over the finish line. She felt disappointed with herself mixed with overwhelm from the questions on the list in front of her. She was in tears, feeling *called* to get her books into the world but having no idea how she'd navigate the world of publishing, even with every step laid out in front of her.

Yet I'm *so* proud of her! And I told her as much. She's gritty and determined and committed. I reminded her of everything she'd accomplished. And asking for help is *part* of the accomplishment! Every book is a team of people invited in at different points to help. She knew just who to ask to get her book over the finish line. Her approach to addressing the procedural block is to hire someone who can do it for her. Great!

This wasn't exactly her mindset around her pivot from DIY to hiring help. She saw it as being "not good enough" or "too old" or "dumb" yet it's actually a sign of her resourcefulness and awareness of the limitations of her time, energy, and skill. That's perfect!

This is what I do with homeschooling. Rather than sitting in a place of helplessness for very long, I lean into my resources. And I have so many! I have quite a few good friends who are homeschooling their kids and are happy to suggest resources. I have a dear friend who has jumped in to help me master math education for my kiddo. I have a liaison at the charter as well as a school counselor that I've learned is available to help me. There are conventions and conferences and podcasts all for people like me. And when I get overwhelmed, I call a friend, I pray, (okay, I also cry), and I might even hire people to take on some of the educating for me. This is not helplessness, this is progress! My kids will have an incredible education not because I have a clue what I'm doing, but because I know how to use the resources available to me to keep them headed toward graduation. Good Lord, have mercy.

Change is exhausting. So is learning.

When we take on a new skill, we start creating new connections and pathways in our brain. As we practice, we strengthen these new connections, which continuously improves how we do the new skill. I think of it like trying to clear a new path in a jungle.

Perhaps there's already a beaten-down path, but poo-throwing monkeys live in the trees and it's just not a great experience. You decide to create a new path to avoid the old one. Problem is, it's *a jungle.* Vines and bushes and brush are natural walls preventing you from just *walking.* So, you grab a machete and begin the arduous task of clearing a new path. You stomp down the brush beneath you, sometimes tripping over a root, getting scratched by thorns, or batting away creatures who've made a home in the cover. But every day you come back, stomping anew on the path you're slowly making, getting a little further in the brush. Until *one day* you turn around and see a *path.* Every day as you've walked the same gritty jungle "road" it adjusted to your presence. You cleared a new pathway by walking over it repeatedly.

You glance at your former path and see that it's become overgrown, hardly recognizable.

This is similar to your brain as it creates new pathways. At first, you experience resistance. It's hard. It keeps wanting to pull back to the familiar, albeit dysfunctional, former path. But the more you train it to beat down the new one, the easier it gets.

This is essentially what it means to start a new habit. A habit is anything you do so repeatedly, like a routine or ritual, that your neurological pathways become deep and resistant to change. Remember, the resistance to change is because it *loves* autopilot! Your brain wants to conserve as much energy as possible for the surprises that might come your way. This is why it's hard to break habits. Once a habit is assigned to autopilot, it's assigned to the basal ganglia of your brain, beneath your conscious control where you develop emotions and memories. This is why you repeat most habits while barely being aware you're even doing them.

But there's more! Not only does your brain love surviving, but it also loves pleasure. I think it's a bit like a bait-and-switch. Your brain dangles the reward of pleasure to direct you toward its perception of survival. But remember, you train your brain! If you've trained its perception of survival, it can begin to reward you for things that are *actually* harmful. We establish the links and cues that our brain uses to determine our approach to living, but most of us allow this to happen passively, with no conscious awareness.

So, a habit is further reinforced when it's linked to a reward. First, we need to recognize the moment we have an opportunity to take a different path (a cue), then we need to know what new path we're taking (action), and our action needs to result in some form of pleasure (reward). These three are the habit-making team.

In other words,

> Habits are actions that are triggered by cues, such as a time of day, an activity, or a location. They culminate in a feel-good reward that, through repetition, fuses the connection between the cue and reward firmly in the brain... You might hit a wall with creative work or a school project and crave a break from the hard mental work. You step outside for a cigarette, both relieving yourself from an uncomfortable situation and giving yourself a nicotine boost. Over time, feeling stuck at work will start to trigger you to reach for cigarettes. Or, that relief might come from something less obviously addictive: scrolling social media. Sound familiar?[1]

The repetition is choosing to walk through the new jungle road every day, even though it's tempting to take the already beaten path. The repetition lets our bodies and brains know this is *important*. It causes our brains to take notice.

I grew up with the saying, "Practice makes perfect." But life taught me that practice makes *permanent*. Perfectly permanent, but that's the only part of "perfect" that actually applies. The more we repeat something, the more we train our bodies that it *matters* and can be set on autopilot. If we "practice" a poor, dysfunctional, harmful habit, we will make that habit *permanent*.

Permanence takes time. Reorganizing your brain as it adjusts to a new skill is an *actual* physical process occurring in your brain. You need time for the repetition to be noted and responded to. Your brain might think, *Oh, I see you, new skill. You look like hard work. I'm not wasting resources on that until I know it's important. So, bye, Felicia.* But then you present that same skill the next day, and the next day, and the next day. Your brain takes notice and says, "A'ight, I gotcha. Let's do this."

But if you quit before your brain is fully convinced, you'll hop right back onto that old jungle path with the fecal-happy monkeys.

CHAPTER TWENTY-FOUR

procedural blocks

THE CHECK ENGINE LIGHT

ENGINE CHECK

A PROCEDURAL BLOCK has a strong association with our habits and our mindset. So how can we tell when the disruption to our creativity is a procedural block? There are a number of symptoms indicated by our check engine light. See if you recognize any of these.

No Follow Through

You may recognize that what you've been doing isn't working. Your book isn't getting written. You rarely even make it to your document, let alone sit and stare at it. You've read articles and books and watched the webinars, but every time you try one of their tips, it doesn't seem to work for you. So, you stay stuck.

No (Self-) Discipline

You may find yourself lacking the basic disciplines of writing. I asked my daughter, "What does not being disciplined mean to you?" because I didn't love the definitions I was finding. She said, "It's not setting rules for yourself and/or not following them." Bam. Exactly.

You might notice this for yourself, a lack of setting rules or standards for yourself and therefore having nothing to follow. It also means not having established a routine or consistency with a routine that matters to you. It's easy here to assign a meaning to this, like my Rebel client who'd set goals only to learn a new instrument instead of writing her book. She had very negative self-talk around her perception of lacking discipline. A lack of discipline in this case isn't a judgment call. We're not pointing fingers here, we're recognizing what's not working, the symptom that surfaces that you can bring your conscious awareness to and *notice.* Do you struggle with "discipline" in lots of life areas?

No Routine

If discipline is the establishment of rules and standards, routine is the path to get there. You may notice that you're great at knowing the "rules" to follow but don't have a plan for getting there. You might struggle with the sequence of actions you need to regularly follow—a routine. Discipline and routine walk hand-in-hand. It's hard to follow a routine if you don't practice discipline! If you notice that you struggle with sticking to a routine or choosing the *right* routine, you're struggling with a procedural block.

Too Many Tools (Or Too Few)

Writing and publishing used to be as simple as needing a quill, ink, and paper. The typewriter introduced a new way of documenting and a new way of reading. Then computers, tablets, and phones entered our world, and everything changed *fast.* Affording these pieces of technology is one thing, but once you *have them*, you learn there's more. You have to navigate which Internet browser to use, which word processor to use, what digital tools are best for formatting, typesetting, and production. You have to learn about email platforms, landing pages, uploading, downloading, and tracking changes... so many things. Some of us have bought or tried *all of the tools* and have tool-overwhelm. Others of us are paralyzed with which tools to choose and then how to use them once we have them. This can definitely inhibit our creative process.

Hamster Wheel

Do you find yourself spinning your wheels and going nowhere at all? This *can* be a sign of a procedural block. When we spend a lot of energy on the wrong habits, routines, workflows, or systems, we spin around without any real progress. You don't know what you don't know! What you *do* know is that you feel busy (researching, learning, guessing, trying) but not making progress. In fact, sometimes this feels like one step forward and two steps back.

These are all symptoms you may notice if you're experiencing a procedural block. As *always,* we assign meaning to our experience with blocks, making our stuckness as much about emotional and mental blocks as procedural blocks. We have to bring our awareness to both. If you find the exact right tool for *you*, it won't support you to its best potential if we haven't also addressed everything beneath the hood. So, let's go there now!

CHAPTER TWENTY-FIVE

procedural blocks

BENEATH THE HOOD

BENEATH THE HOOD

It's easy to recognize the fact that you *want* to write your book but *aren't.* It's much harder to understand *why* you're not making progress. When you're willing to direct your attention to the deeper issues standing in your way, you'll make progress. Like the author I shared above—she recognized she wasn't making the progress she wanted *and* knew exactly what was in her way: technology. On our call together, we were able to dig even deeper and address the feelings she had about her struggle with technology. We *truthfully* shifted her perception from "I'm too old for this," to, "I know how to meet my needs to get my important book into the world." Huge!

Have you ever tried to pull a weed up from the ground? It's so satisfying when the *whole* weed comes up, root and all. But sometimes only the top breaks off... and the weed grows right back because the roots remained in the dirt. Stupid weeds. We need to get to the root of our procedural blocks, internal messages and all, if we want to know the exact right tip that will unblock us and get our stories into the world.

Now let's take a look at a few of the root causes. Some of these will seem familiar because roots are roots. How they appear on the surface may have some distinction (i.e., a dandelion or crabgrass) but beneath the ground is a web of roots that all need to be addressed.

Delaying the Inevitable

This root has surfaced a number of different weeds. We've seen it with a fear of closure/goodbye. We've seen it with a fear of other people's opinions and a fear of rejection or retribution. Our fear of the unknown can show up in procedural blocks too. "I don't know whether to use Word or Google Docs" is an easy excuse to justify not making progress on your book. It's easy but unacceptable. That's why we address it. If you notice that you're using procedural blocks as a reason to be stuck, stop and ask yourself, "*Why?*" You have the resources you need (here and in other places) to answer every procedural question you have. If you're not utilizing those resources, you might be delaying the inevitable. Ask yourself why and let's pull that root out! (Then if you still want to know whether Google Docs or Word is better, see "Grab the Wrench" in the next chapter.)

I'm being generous to say "inevitable." It's my belief in you that publishing your book and putting it into the world is inevitable. Some people never see their stories in the hands of the world and their legacy dies with them, buried beneath a lifetime of dreams they never saw realized. That's not you. I can tell because you're here. So, it's inevitable that you will put your book into the world, people will read it, and have thoughts about it. This is as exhilarating as it is terrifying.

Let me take your hand and say, "It's all going to be okay. In fact, it's going to be amazing. All those butterflies in your tummy? They get excited when you bravely step into the unknown because you believe in your story. They know what transformation feels like, and the beauty that follows. They can't wait for you to see it too."

Sometimes their flutters make us want to delay leaving the cozy cocoon. Sometimes we interpret those flutters as fear. But nope.

Those flutters anticipate *all* of the good that's coming because you chose courage. Those flutters are the cheering squad of the already changed who champion you across that finish line so you can join their ranks.

Tech-Challenged and Dumb

It's amazing to me how many people have assigned messages of limited intelligence to their ability to understand technology. Let's remember that not only is technology still relatively new in the context of all of time, but it's *always changing.* I think of myself as tech-capable, but *man,* there are days when everything feels new (because it is!). New software, phone upgrades, AI... the world is changing faster than any of us can keep up with, yet we judge ourselves for the struggle. Stop it.

Many of my authors have self-sabotaged their dream to avoid the beast of technology. And let me tell you, many of them wouldn't have written a book, let alone published it, if they hadn't invited people like me or Gary or other services who *have* the tech skill. *And that's okay.* But some people allow such shame to attach to their lack of tech skills that they trigger their survival brain and run for the hills. If that person feels *called* to tell their story, then shame piles upon shame. They perceive their weakness to be the reason they'll fail God or the world for not getting their story onto shelves. Holy Moly! That's huge! Who wants to fail the divine *and* the whole world? Cue all the sabotages to making progress on the book. I've known authors to self-edit a perfectly-ready-for-an-editor manuscript for *years* just to avoid what's coming next... technology.

If there's any failure in the tech-challenged experience, it's not inviting help when you need it. It's nursing a belief that the only way to write and publish is *by yourself.* A belief that help is failure is wacky at best and totally destructive at worst. If you find yourself feeling overwhelmed with the technology needed to publish, stop and ask yourself what messages are coming up for you. Then make a list of all the resources you can utilize to tackle those tech pieces. I know beautiful people who help authors with done-*for*-you and done-*with*-you services to get your book up and over the tech hurdles. Add them to your list of resources.

Lack of Self Awareness

Yep, here we are again. Not knowing ourselves is a culprit behind many obstacles we face, but especially here. Feel free to review this section in Scarcity Blocks, but here we're going to address it through the lens of the habits and systems and tools we choose.

Not every habit or system is going to work for *you*. For example, this tip works for many people: Put writing time in your calendar. Treat it like an appointment. Don't allow anything to double book with your scheduled writing time. Put your butt in the chair just like you would if you were in the doctor's office. Use alarms if you need reminders. I've known many authors to use this suggestion and resolve a block. I was sure, because it worked for so many people, that it would work for me. So, I scheduled all the writing times. And do you know what happened? Nothing. No writing. My brain knew that it *wasn't* a doctor's appointment and therefore refused to treat it like one. I double-booked if something important came up (which was just about any time anyone needed anything from me). You see, the doctor *expects* me to come, but my book doesn't. It wasn't until I learned more about *me* that I realized why that tip doesn't work for me. I'd just assumed something was wrong with *me,* because it clearly worked for everyone else. I was the only difference.

But then I learned that I need greater accountability for my own goals than just an inanimate calendar. I need someone to expect it of me. So, when my business manager told me to put my writing time in my calendar, we both knew it wouldn't be enough. To further support myself, I gave him access to my calendar. His *eyes* are always on what I'm *supposed* to be doing and he reaches out to make sure. We also jokingly/not-jokingly added to my calendar events "Don't double book or (insert motivational threat)." I value the thing being threatened, and since I know he can see my calendar and follow through on the "threat," I'm way more motivated to honor those scheduled times.

I realized I'm not dumb or broken or defective because the calendar doesn't work for me (by itself). I learned that as an Obliger I need external accountability, that as an INFP I need to feel in alignment with the project I'm working on, that as an Enneagram 9 I will struggle to prioritize myself but will be motivated to serve others, and that as *Marcy* I love working on a team, even in my own business. ALL of this removes any opportunity for shame and enables me to find the habits and strategies that work for *me*. You need to find the ones that work for you. Not knowing yourself well enough means you'll try every tip thrown at you indiscriminately and potentially spend a great deal of time judging yourself (or the tip-giver) for the ones that don't work for you. Study *you* and you'll recognize immediately the habits and systems you'll need to fill your unique gaps.

Not That Committed

Hold on! Don't judge either of us before you hear what I have to say about this. Not being committed is a red flag, not an accusation. It's like getting beneath the hood and finding oil in places you shouldn't. It's deeper than the "check engine" light but not as deep as you'll need to go. Finding yourself lacking commitment to your writing is an opportunity to ask *really good* questions. What is the root of lacking commitment? Are you writing the *wrong* book? Do you need to step back and ask, "Is this the book I'm supposed to be writing right now?" Sometimes our lack of commitment is actually a sign that we're out of alignment somehow. It may be the *right* book but the *wrong* structure. I've lost interest in a book I'm writing when *how* I'm writing it doesn't feel *right*. But if I don't stop to consider *why* it's not right, I'll just keep avoiding writing. Pulling back and reviewing my outline or story structure and making adjustments, even major ones, can renew my commitment and get me going again.

I was recently hired by an author to do the copyediting for her adult nonfiction book. Once I opened the book, however, I quickly realized that her development editor had either lacked the skill or knowledge of story development or been lazy in their feedback. Regardless of the reason, no one was going to read her book. She had *way* too much exposition (back story) before getting to the promise of her book. I was caught between her expectation (that she was almost done and only needed a copyedit) and the reality that loving the author and championing her journey meant being honest about what her book needed. I gave her two options: I could copyedit, *or* I could suggest some major changes that would greatly improve her book but take more time. Fortunately, she managed her disappointment and was all in for the better version of her book.

When we finished *all* of the edits, she said, "I can't thank you enough for taking this project on when your schedule has been so full. You have challenged me and made this manuscript transform from good to great. Like you, I am praying this book blesses many and will encourage others..." Seeing her book transform through adjustments to the structure renewed her commitment and excitement. She was now sharing a *great* book, not just a good one. Facing "delays" to get realigned with our book and writing is well worth it.

Pro Tip: While we're on the topic, do *not* waste energy being upset about delays. Delays have a purpose. They're important. If you have to delay your book launch by two weeks or two months in order for it to be the *best* version of itself, then do it! No reader is out there thinking, "If that book doesn't come out on December first, then I'm not reading it." Trust the timing, even when it veers from the plan you had. Of course, aim for your deadlines! But allow flexibility when they shift. In the case of the above-mentioned author, she had enough wiggle room in her schedule that my work didn't delay her publishing process at all.

On the other hand, my first book, *Reclaiming Hope: Overcoming the Challenges of Parenting Foster and Adopted Children,* faced delay after delay. The formatting came back wonky multiple times and needed to be fixed. I had to adjust my launch date and felt so discouraged. It ended up getting pushed back enough that it landed squarely in November's National Adoption Month, which I hadn't even realized existed until my publishing landed in it. I realized how the delays had actually set me up for this brilliant convergence. I had wasted energy on frustration and stress rather than trusting the process to work for my good. Now I know better!

So, your lack of commitment may be that you're out of alignment with the actual story being told, how you're telling your story, or the timing of your story. Pay attention (directional) to where the lack of commitment is stemming from and ask yourself good questions. I believe that even starting a book that doesn't get published is *so* important for the book that *will be* published. Nothing is wasted. Everything you poured into the first attempt was like clearing the stones from the topsoil to plant what you're supposed to plant. The process of checking in with your commitment is *crucial.*

Now it's time to grab the wrench and get to work! The next chapter is *full* to the brim with tips for kicking those procedural blocks to the curb!

CHAPTER TWENTY-SIX

procedural blocks

GRAB THE WRENCH

GRAB THE WRENCH

You guys, this is the moment I've been waiting for. I *love* helping people overcome procedural blocks. Sometimes the slightest shift in how we do things can change everything. Don't get me wrong, I get a special pleasure when someone has a deep, iceberg-level "aha" that shifts their self-messaging, reveals their value, mirrors their true selves, and empowers them, not just to write an incredible book, but to live an incredible life. I could die today with tremendous satisfaction knowing that I've been a small piece in someone's puzzle to writing their story. But since I'm still alive, I'll keep laying puzzle pieces down, hoping you find the one elusive piece you've been needing for your next step.

PRO TIPS FOR HABITS

Habits: a regular tendency or practice that is repeated regularly.

Remember that your brain has a kind of "muscle memory." The more we utilize its responsiveness to change, the more we can learn, grow, and expand.

There are great books, like James Clear's book *Atomic Habits*, where you can have an entire resource devoted to just habit-building. I want to throw a few of my own ideas in here as well, but definitely utilize a trusted resource that focuses on the whole of a topic if you *know* that's what you need.

Create Associations: Your brain loves to make connections. Use that to your advantage! There are a few different ways you can do this. Choose the ones that make the most sense for *you*. Then customize them to suit your brain's reward center. For example, a Coke (cue) wouldn't capture my attention (craving) therefore I'd carry on my merry way (action) and experience nothing notable (reward). A Pepsi (especially a Roy Rogers) (cue) would definitely capture my attention (crave), especially with real cherries crowding the top. I'd say, "Yes, please!" and happily pay for it with money or writing or whatever (action) to experience the happiness of my taste buds and the association I have with my childhood (reward). So, what may motivate me won't necessarily motivate you. Choose your association.

What you want to do is choose a few things you can use to dangle in front of your brain to say, "Hey, Brain! It's writing time!" You need to create distinctions for your brain of writing/creating time from any other time. That means choosing associations that you can limit to your writing time.

For example, I used to drink a Cherry Pepsi and eat a salty snack every time I wrote and accidentally created an association (worked great for my writing but not my booty). I didn't know about brain associations back then... I just knew I liked Cherry Pepsi and salty things and happened to give them to myself when I wrote. Before long, two things happened. First, drinking Cherry Pepsi and eating salty snacks *made* me want to write, no matter what I was doing.

Second, when I sat down to write, my brain said, "Hey, you want me to be creative? Give me the goods." I had created an association that was powerful (if also unhealthy).

This leads me to **Habit Swapping**. This is where we trade a poor habit for something better. It didn't take long to realize that I needed a healthier alternative to Cherry Pepsi and salty snacks if I was going to be a career writer. I couldn't dump the whole gig cold turkey because my brain was attached, and I'd potentially lose my ability to write for a bit while I began a new association. Instead, I swapped one habit for a new one while keeping the others present. This was less disruptive to my brain. I began by trading my Cherry Pepsi for an herbal tea with raw honey (my favorite). Totally different drink, but because my other associations were still in place (I'll get to those in a sec), my brain pouted a tiny bit, but then got straight back to creating. I eventually turned my salty snack into a healthy snack, keeping my groove while slowly swapping better habits for poor habits, but not losing the momentum of my writing.

Habit Stacking is another way to create new habits without disrupting your brain's associations too much. According to James Clear,[1] author of *Atomic Habits*, Habit Stacking is taking a habit you already have, any habit, and attaching your new habit to it. There are a bunch of things you do every day without thinking about it. Perhaps that's taking a shower, brushing your teeth, making coffee, going for a run, getting into bed, checking the mirror, or whatever! Now, take that no-brainer habit and attach your new habit to it.

Clear lays out the Habit Stacking formula like this:

After/Before [*CURRENT HABIT*], *I will* [*NEW HABIT*].

After I shower, I will write for thirty minutes.

After I make my Chai Latte, I will write one thousand words.

After I take my kids to school, I will free write until lunch.

> Again, the reason habit stacking works so well is that your current habits are already built into your brain. You have patterns and behaviors that have been strengthened over years. By linking your new habits to a cycle that is already built into your brain, you make it more likely that you'll stick to the new behavior. Once you have mastered this basic structure, you can begin to create larger stacks by chaining small habits together. This allows you to take advantage of the natural momentum that comes from one behavior leading into the next.[2]

Habit Pairing. Yep, there's another one, Habit Pairing. This is similar to habit stacking, except instead of one following the other, you can combine them or use one as the reward. For example, maybe you love watching Netflix but are really trying to get more physically active. Habit Pairing would mean bringing your treadmill in front of your show and doing both together. If you already have a habit of watching a show, you can *pair it* with your new habit, running on the treadmill. Another example of this would be to take your favorite podcasts to the pavement with you. Choose to *only* listen to your favorite podcasts when you're out walking or running.

I recently used a regular commute to begin voice recording the next section of my book, then used a service like Otter to transcribe it when I wasn't driving. I paired one habit (my commute) with a new habit (speak-to-text-ing my book)!

This is pairing your habits and using one as a kind of simultaneous reward for the other. This has the added benefit of creating a reward sensation with your new habit, further reinforcing its importance to your brain.

You can also use other environmental factors to create an association between your brain and writing time. You can use smells, sights, and tastes (like I accidentally did with Cherry Pepsi and salty yummies).

Whatever you choose, only use that *thing* during your writing time. This solidifies to your brain that it's time to write.

I love using candles. I have a special writing candle. I only light it when I'm writing. As soon as my brain catches a whiff, it's like a happy puppy wagging a furiously excited tail. "Oooh, ooh, I know this one!" My brain rolls over for a belly rub every time and we have the *best* time writing together. Consider using an aroma to create an association between your brain and writing. Remember, your brain *loves* to use the least amount of energy possible, so the more you can help it out, the better for both of you.

You can also use a music playlist. I use an Instrumental Covers playlist on Spotify. I can't listen to music with words and stay focused, so I chose instrumental. My brain is *so* familiar with the playlist that as soon as the first chord of the first song starts playing, it's down to writing business. (Yes, it's playing even now.)

You can use almost anything. You can choose to sit in the same spot every time you write. Ideally, you only sit there when writing, but even the consistency of showing up to the same spot regardless will have an associative impact.

Or you can do it all! Music, candle, location... the more you give your brain, the better, and the easier if you need to swap a habit later like I did! Not only was the swap between Cherry Pepsi and tea relatively minor, but I still had my music, my aroma, and my location to keep my brain from too much disruption in the swap.

Be intentional. Choose one to a few things you can build into your writing time to create an association between your brain and creativity. Try a smell, time, location, sound, or ambiance and see what works.

Now, remember, *starting* a new association is like running your first mile. The first time you light a candle your brain will dismiss it. There's no connection. You'll still need to write with your beautiful aroma and struggle to write like any other time. But every time you sit, light that candle and it *will* catch on.

Which leads to another habit-building tip. ***Just. Start. Writing.*** I mentioned this before but treat your initial sitting as that first painful mile of a run. Or like sitting in your garden and removing the stones and weeds. Both situations require that you demonstrate patience in doing the yucky-feeling thing to get to the reward. Remember, any of the "weeds" you write during this first "mile" can be tossed later, but you need to let them OUT to get to the good stuff. Habit-building is the perseverance you demonstrate to your brain about *hard things*. You teach yourself and your brain that you are a person who pushes through the hard things because you *know* the good is just around the corner. And it is! You can't edit a blank page. You can't plant your garden without removing some of the ground cover. It's part of the process. Once you accept that, writing junk to get to the gems won't bother you at all. In fact, it will excite you.

This is how some of my "first mile" writing goes.

"I have no idea what to say. I'm supposed to be writing an article on my confession that I like to eat three eggs sometimes. But I don't know where to take it. I'm distracted and bored and... blank. I don't want to write about eggs. But I know this will help people. I *know* that I'm not the only one who has false messages that have held me back. I know that talking about the shame that rises up in me when I think of eating three eggs instead of two will help others with body dysmorphia or faulty thinking around health and nutrition to feel encouraged. They'll know they're not alone and we can talk about it..."

And before I know it, I'm writing my article. Yep, I'm going to have to delete the junk at the front and massage the intro, but writing *anything*, especially writing about my stuckness, leads me to a flow that will carry me for quite a while. Sometimes my "first mile" writing actually takes me down another path. It might be that I need to process something else *first.* Maybe I need to talk about how overwhelmed I've been feeling, or how what a friend said the other day stung and I can't shake it. But I won't know what's in my way until I let myself pull up the weeds. It's *always* worth it. Just start.

My last thought on habit-building tips is to mind your messages! Your brain believes what you say (most of the time). If you say, "I'm a horrible writer; I can't do this," your brain believes you! It then wants to divert as much energy *away* from your writing as possible. Why waste precious resources on something you suck at? Turn that talk around and say, "Every first draft is rough. Even Brené Brown and Anne Lamott say so. This just shows that I'm an author! I can definitely do this."

Sometimes we have to say things for our brain's sake while we're on our way to believing them. That's okay, as long as it's positive and supports you. Make a list of positive messages or affirmations that you can speak aloud to yourself. Hang them around your writing space. Read them and choose to believe them.

I've even borrowed the belief of trusted friends. I had no idea if I was actually capable of running a business, let alone getting my book published. But each step of the way I was surrounded by cheerleaders who believed in me. I borrowed that belief for a long time, and it worked! So, borrow my belief if you need to. I don't need to have met you in person yet, I already believe in you. Because I believe *every voice* matters and I'm all about getting yours into the world. Someone needs it. I need it. And I know you have everything you need to make it happen. So, **borrow belief** if you have to.

Okay, let's talk about tips related to your systems.

PRO TIPS FOR SYSTEMS

System: the tools that you use to get your writing down.

Are you feeling tech-challenged? Are you confused about where or how to write your book? This is your section. Let's go!

"Where do I even write the book?" You've spent a *lot* of time asking and researching this question. And guess what? The answer is to use whatever software you've been using! Now, if you haven't been using any, you get to start! This does *not* have to be complicated. Really. The priority is your comfort and convenience, and then the ease of your editor accessing and editing your work when it's time. Here are some options.

Microsoft Word or Pages are the standard word processors that come with your computer depending on whether you use an Apple device or not. They work similarly. When purchasing a computer, you'll want to make sure that a word processor is included (they aren't always!). Word usually comes in a Microsoft package of some sort, so make sure your computer came with it. These are word processors that are applications on your device, so if your computer dies, you lose your files. Some of these processors have a backup option provided that uses the Internet. A file created by Pages or Word is saved to your computer and shared via email or other file-sharing tools like Dropbox. Make sure to regularly save your document as you write so you don't lose your progress if the battery dies or something glitches. This is rare but worth the effort if you end up in a situation!

Google Docs is an online word processor. That means it is not an app stored on your computer. You can access it from anywhere you can access the Internet. If your computer dies, your document remains untouched online. You can also easily share your document by adding someone's email to the share option and choosing what level of access they can have. Google Docs auto-saves your work as you write and retains a history of changes should you ever need to go back in time and undo something. Multiple people can work in the same document at the same time, and it will show you what's happening. As far as utility, it allows you to do most of the things you would do in Word or Pages. Some editors won't accept a Google Doc, in which case you can export your document into a Word document and send it that way.

Again, use the word processor you're already using. If you haven't been using one, just pick one and start with it. You can't go wrong with any of the above-mentioned processors.

I'll sum up this part with a short mention of Scrivener. I get asked about it a lot. In fact, I'm using it right now. But I don't recommend it to beginning writers. It's like the behemoth of word processors. It can do a million things... and that's part of the problem. I probably only use seven percent of what it offers, but I love that seven percent. Still, at the end of the day, I eventually pull it out of Scrivener and put it on Pages (because I have a Mac). If you're looking for an over-the-top robust word processor and you're already very familiar with the other options, then you can consider Scrivener. Otherwise, pretend it doesn't exist for now.

"I hate writing. Can I speak a book?"

This is a question that many people have but not many ask. Yes! You can definitely speak your book. Most word processors now have an accessibility option for that. On Pages, it's under "Start Dictation" (as of this writing). You can speak to your computer, and it will write the words down for you without you having to type them. In fact, I just did that with this sentence. You can do the same in Word with the "Dictate" feature. In Google Docs, the feature is called "Voice Typing." You can also record a voice note on your phone (or anywhere else you can record a voice note or video) and submit it to a platform like Otter.ai. Otter will transcribe your voice note or video and give you the transcript. They have a free option and a paid option. Dragon (Dictation) is another company that offers dictation services. Some authors have spoken their entire book!

"My editor said to track changes. What in the world does that mean?"

As an editor myself, I *love* when authors know how to use tracked changes. Tracked changes is a feature in all of the word processors that allows me (the editor) to show you (the author) what changes I've made. It shows up in a different color. I can leave comments (which are visible in the margin) to which you can respond. In Google Docs, this is called "Suggesting" versus "Tracked Changes." I prefer this in my editing work so you can 1) see the changes I'm making and learn from them and 2) make decisions about the changes being made. As an author, I love seeing what the editor has done as opposed to getting a book back and being clueless about what's changed. It's a way of replicating the red pen you might have grown up with on your childhood essays.

Your job as the author is to go through and resolve the changes. You can do that by choosing to accept or reject the change. If you reject the change, it's undone. If you accept it, it releases the "hold" on it as a suggestion and includes the edit.

Now, when it's time for *you* to make changes, it's important to keep the tracked changes *on*. This allows your editor to see what you've added and changed so they can pay special attention to the new pieces you've added or adjusted. It's a form of conversation and keeps everyone on the same page (ha!).

If you're unsure how to find "tracked changes" or "suggestions" in your word processor, try a Google search. There are some great tutorials.

PRO TIPS FOR WORKFLOW

Workflow is the *way* you work, the sequence or processes through which a piece of work passes from initiation to completion.

Sometimes you can have solid habits and a great handle on the technology for writing and still struggle with procedural blocks. That means this section should give you a boost!

The first thing to remember is to pace yourself. Choose to **touch your book *every day***. Even if it's just opening your manuscript and re-reading what you wrote last and adding one sentence. Sometimes we get it into our heads that writing time has to be an hour or more. We look at our calendars, shake our heads, and think, *I guess I'll get back to it next week.*

This is crazy! You *will* eventually write a book, even if it's one minute at a time, one sentence at a time. You will *not* write a book by waiting for the right hour to come along sometime next week. It won't come. Or at least not enough of them will come to finish your book. Books get written by deciding to write the next sentence with any minutes you're given. Some days are so full! Touch your book anyway. The more time that passes between book touches, the less motivation you have to return to it, and the harder it is to get back in the seat to move your book forward.

Sometimes we avoid the daily touches because of overwhelm. Much of our overwhelm comes from jumping into the future (anything beyond the next three seconds) and imagining the *what ifs*, and there are many! Your brain and body don't travel with you into the future, they stay in the present. So, when you allow your thoughts to wander into the great beyond, it's *all a made-up story*. Yet your body reacts as though you are actually living the horrific possibilities you're fearing. This leads to your heart rate increasing, your breath going shallow, and overwhelm. It shuts you down.

Which is the next tip. **Stay present.** Time-hopping doesn't serve you or your story.

I love the story of a man who was gifted an ant farm. One of my clients told me about her friend who was about to head out on vacation but was handed this random gift (who gives ant farms? It's never even crossed my mind to do so). He left it on his desk and forgot about it. I mean, it was just a bunch of dirt squished between two plastic walls.

When he returned from his holiday, the ant farm caught his eye. It had morphed from a wall of dirt into an intricate city of tunnels, brimming with life and beauty. It was organized and tremendous. He got close to watch the ants working and noticed they were doing this work by moving *one piece of sand at a time.*

How many of us have looked at the huge project in front of us and said, "Nope." It seemed too big. Yet how do we move a mountain? One stone at a time. How do we eat an elephant? (Yuck) One bite at a time.

And how do you make a city of tunnels as one of the teeniest creatures on earth?

By moving one piece of sand at a time.

By writing the next word.

Friend, that is all you have to do. Move your piece of sand. Just one. The next one.

And take breaks.

Many of us live in a society that prizes busyness. And if we're not trying to earn the busyness ribbon, we're using busyness to drown out our uncomfortable thoughts, memories, and feelings.

Then you sit at your computer and can't understand why nothing is coming out. Or you sit to write... and write and write and eventually burn your brain out. Don't get me wrong, a good writing groove can last a long time, and pausing can feel like a horrible idea if you're in a good flow! But your brain does actually have a limited capacity for efficient processing. Breaks allow your brain to revitalize.

Studies have shown that for about every twenty to thirty minutes of focused learning, you should take a three- to five-minute brain break.

By "break" I don't mean you have to stare at a wall. A brain break is shifting between brain networks, using different parts of it allows other parts to rest and refresh. So, if you've been writing for a while, pause and go put your feet in the grass. Feel the coolness. Let the sun or rain or snow touch your face and *feel* it. Stretch, sing, dance, interact with another human... do something different, then get back to your writing![3]

Your writing process should include touching your manuscript every day, staying present, doing the next thing, and taking brain breaks.

It also helps to have a plan. Your plan might look different from mine, and that's great! (Have I mentioned yet how important it is to know yourself?) My writing process is to notice a theme rising up in me that I want to share with others. If it *keeps* coming up, I consider whether it's supposed to be an article, a presentation I give, or a book I write. Most of my ideas do not become books. Most of my ideas come from years of conversations, years of my brain noticing patterns and wondering if what I see can help others. The idea might come in the form of a book title (I see book titles in everything) or a concept.

When I finally get to the realization that it's supposed to be a book, I grab the largest whiteboard I can find and brain-dump everything I can think of related to the topic. Some people use lots of sticky notes. Others use online brainstorming software. Find what works for you!

Once my brain feels rather empty, I begin to focus on the connections I see. I use colors to circle the words or sentences that have something in common, and from this, create chapters or sections of an outline. People who use sticky notes will gather the notes into groupings of themes. From this brain-dump, I'll form an outline, first loosely, and eventually with detail. I'll put as much detail in my outline as possible, including quotes, keywords, whatever. That way when I begin writing, I already have a lot of content. I also have the most productive writing experience when I repeat this process for *each chapter*. Brainstorm, outline, write. This works for me but not everyone.

Some people need less planning and more writing. They're able to write straight from the organization of their thoughts. An outline feels restrictive to them. Other people need even more detailed outlines than I do. The important thing is that you know the map of your own process or workflow and follow it. When I deviate from my best workflow (thinking, *I've written eighteen books, I don't need to brainstorm each chapter.*) I end up on tangents, forgetting what I was writing about to begin with, confusing myself, and, without good editing, confusing my readers too. I've learned I need to stick with my workflow. It works for me.

You might be more of a mosaic writer instead of a linear writer. You'll hear most gurus say, "No! Don't hop around! Write in order!" But why? If it works better for your brain to write pieces in different places as you go, then scrap the advice and do *you*. Write like you'd create a mosaic. The goal is progress.

Some people find that setting a word-count goal each day gets them lit up and writing. Others find that they need a time goal, and then write fast and furious while the clock ticks.

Some writers join challenges like National Novel Writing Month (NaNoWriMo), Storystorm for picture books, or my own Start Your Story or Idea to Draft challenges. They find that the accountability, timeframe, and communal participation give them the oomph they need to get going. Other writers have tried a challenge only to find themselves overwhelmed and discouraged.

Find what works for you. It might go against conventional wisdom and advice. Who cares? If it works for you, do it. If I say you need to touch your book every day but writing in five-hour bursts each weekend works best for you, then ignore me and go do it!

Which leads to my final tip: **Give yourself permission to do *you*.**

Take any advice in this book (or any book, article, TED talk (yep), webinar, guru, etc.) and dump what doesn't work for *you*. Take what partially works and mold it into something that supports you. If something works, then hold it, love it, take care of it, and write your beautiful heart out. We need your words. Don't let any advice deter or confuse you. Remember, what works for one person won't work for everyone. This is true in parenting, romantic partnerships, business, and basically all of life.

CHAPTER TWENTY-SEVEN

procedural blocks

BACK ON THE ROAD

GET BACK ON THE ROAD

It's time to stop looking at that blinking cursor, unsure of what to say. Stop scrolling TikTok or YouTube or staring at your bedroom wall. An hour later, guess what? You'll still have the same blinky cursor and the same NO WORDS behind it. You have everything you need to get going. And if you didn't find the answer here, you know where to find it! I'm happy to consult with you or direct you to someone or a resource that will keep you going. *You* are the only thing standing between where you are now and where you want to be.

So, grab the procedural block tips that make the best sense *for you* and get going! It's time to get back on the road.

> *The secret of getting ahead is getting started. The secret of getting started is breaking your complex overwhelming tasks into small manageable tasks, and then starting on the first one.*
>
> —Mark Twain

"You don't start out writing good stuff. You start out writing crap and thinking it's good stuff, and then gradually you get better at it. That's why I say one of the most valuable traits is persistence."

—Octavia Butler

CHAPTER TWENTY-EIGHT

conclusion

WE'VE all stared at a blank page. And we've all judged ourselves for it. We've been stuck, uninspired, given in to the voice of the imposter, doubted ourselves, and maybe even quit. But if you're here, and I'm here, then we have chosen to un-quit.

You picked up this book because you believed it might hold what you need to turn that blinking cursor into a phoenix rising from the ashes of writer's block.

We've geeked out on the brain, addressed what writer's block *really is*, and been filled to the brim with ideas for overcoming obstacles through the five main blockages: Mental, Emotional, Scarcity, Attentional, and Procedural.

Wow, we've covered a lot. We've taken a deep dive into the psychology of creative blocks, and you've hung in there.

You can use this book like a "Choose Your Own Block Breaker." Come back and choose the section that seems to be most in your way and try one of the tips! It's a book that keeps giving. That's how I like it.

You're also welcome to join me in *The Writer's Block*, the community I host full of writers and illustrators committed to getting their books written and published. I provide monthly group coaching calls, access to expert interviews, a community of dedicated people, and all of the resources and recommendations you need to go from start to finish. I'd love to have you.

Wherever your author journey takes you, know that I'm cheering you on. Your voice matters. Your story matters. You are stronger than every obstacle that comes against you. Just because you're strong doesn't mean the load isn't heavy. But heavy develops muscles and those muscles will carry you through your current book project, your next book, and any other life changes that meet you along the way.

Many writers think that the journey is getting their book onto shelves. That's definitely a great part of the journey, but it's only one piece of it.

Writing is about self-discovery, resilience, healing, and becoming more than you ever imagined you can be. I see you, writer.

Thank you for bravely walking the road so many have given up on before.

If this book has been a helpful part of your journey, I'd love to know! Please reach out and share your "aha" story. What helped dislodge you and get you moving again? I'd love to celebrate with you.

Here's to changing our world, one word at a time.

Remember to grab your free guide to publishing, all the way from writing your book through post-launch tips. Gathered from hundreds of publishing experiences as a publishing press as well as an award-winning author. Grab it free!

Do you want the guide for children's authors? Grab it here: miramarepontepress.com/publish

miramarepontepress.com/publishing-checklist

QUICK REFERENCE GUIDE

MENTAL BLOCKS

Ever been impacted by someone else's story? They felt like an imposter too. Remember that and put words on that page. You're the only one who can.

The best way to overcome perfectionism is to practice imperfection.

Be intentional about the thoughts you think. Do *something* to give your RAS a new thought or belief to reinforce.

If you find yourself thinking that you can't move forward until you have more information, try one of these:

- Do the *very next thing* that you *can* do.
- Ask someone who knows what you need to know. Sometimes asking for guidance *is* the next step, so take it.
- Pause, set a timer for fifteen or thirty minutes, and research your heart out. Then get back to writing.
- If you're writing fiction, try asking your character! Find a set of interview questions, from simple things you'll never use in your story, to the big questions you have. Ask your character and then write whatever comes to mind.
- Role-play the character interview with someone else.

Take time to love the little child inside of you who still needs a hug, reassurance, and a reminder that they're seen, heard, and valued. Do something kind for yourself today that you'd only do for someone you really love and value.

When you hear yourself thinking that you're behind, pause and dig deeper. How do you know you're "behind?" Who says? Adjust your expectations as needed. *Keep moving forward.*

If you're trying to hit a writing or publishing goal, then either make a plan to hit your goal or adjust your goal. It's okay to publish your book a week or a month later than you thought. If that causes any anxiety in you, then pause and ask why. Challenge the answer that rises to the surface.

EMOTIONAL BLOCKS

Ask yourself, "What's the story I've believed about failure? What do I think it's saying about me? What am I worried people will think about me? Why?" Keep digging deeper. If your answer is, "Failure says I'm a worthless loser," then ask yourself, "Why? Is it true?"

*When you hear a false narrative (and you will, all sorts of them), listen for the helplessness. Choose to show your brain why you are *not* helpless.

> "Brain, I know you can't see right now how I'll know (or afford) what to do next, but we'll cross that bridge when we get there. What I *do* know is that I'm capable, resourceful, and smart. I've gotten this far using those very traits. When I get to the next obstacle, I may not know the solution, but I know how to take a single step toward one. I've got this."

You can even go deeper if you're sensing you need it... and give your brain examples of what you'll do.

> "I know Marcy helps writers, so I'll contact her. See, Brain? We've got some great connections who will help us keep moving forward."

You can do this through an actual conversation, letter writing, journaling, role-playing with a trusted friend, a doodle, whatever! As soon as your brain feels secure that you don't need to be stuck in a "freeze" state, you'll be released back into parts of your brain that allow you to move forward in the best possible ways.

If you're staring at a blank screen or bored by your own writing, pause. Ask yourself,

> "What areas of my heart still need a little attention? What can I do to dislodge my unprocessed pain?"

Consider grabbing some Play-Doh and letting your hands create. Don't plan it, script it, or think about it, just mold the Play-Doh into *something*.

When you feel complete, hold that thing in your hand. Ask your creation, "What would you like me to know?" and listen. Journal the thoughts that come to mind or speak them out loud to yourself. Bring your curiosity to your creation.

If you see something you don't understand, ask about it. "What's the little bumpy part right here? Tell me about that," and notice what you hear.

Then allow yourself to respond. What do *you* want your creation to know? You can go back and forth as many times as you'd like until you and your creation both feel heard. This is a surprisingly simple yet powerful sensory activity that can begin healing the parts of your wounded heart that need attention.

You can also create a collage, draw or paint a picture, beat on a drum (or drum-like thing), or move your body the way it wants to move (remember, uncensored!). Then try writing again and see if anything has shifted!

Gather a trusted group of champions and keep them close. Find your people. Vet them (not just anyone is allowed that privileged seat). Start with one and go from there. Find safe, trusted communities if you need one to get started (this might be a focus group around the kind of emotional or relational injury you experienced. There are groups for victims of abuse and crimes, divorce groups, parenting groups, singles groups, addiction, veteran's groups, on and on). Find a belonging space and *be* a belonging space. This will help you navigate the opinions of others, determine windows from mirrors, and initiate an important salve to your relational injuries.

Have a book launch party where you pause to celebrate the "graduation" of your book from the nest to the world! Not only does it provide an opportunity to announce and sell your book, gather people, and throw a party, but it allows you to embody and experience a very important "rite of passage" for your book. This can help your brain make peace with the change and open up to new possibilities.

SCARCITY BLOCKS

Know who you are writing for and how you hope to impact them. Are you writing for children? Then picture those children, picture their lives without your book. Picture your life before you found your favorite most impactful book. Don't withhold that from them by nursing a misunderstanding around your access to time. Give your story to the world.

When you hear the message inside your head, "I don't have enough money. I can't afford my dream," pause and begin to brainstorm possibilities for solving that problem. Pull out a sheet of paper or a note on your phone. Ask a friend to hop on a call to brainstorm with you, throw it on the Internet and see what feedback you get. You don't have to rely on the limitations of your brain and experiences. Lean into that of others and see what ideas come up for you. Maybe it's a fundraiser, maybe it's a presale, maybe it's a line of credit, maybe it's taking on a side job or monetizing a hobby. The money is there and available to you. Will you go get it? Do you believe in your dream? Do you believe in your book? If you don't believe in it, no one else will either. This is an opportunity to show yourself what you are capable of.

When you notice a feeling of helplessness in your mind or your body as you think about everything you don't know, pause and ask yourself *who* do you know? Do you know anyone who's published before? Do you know anyone with connections to someone who's published? Have you watched a webinar with someone you came to trust, who demonstrated they can fill your knowledge gaps? Reach out!

Knowing yourself is *lifelong* so pace yourself. Start with *one tool.* You can start with an easy, free assessment like the Four Tendencies. You can join a community like the one I'm part of, the Changemaker community, where we meet bi-monthly to dig into who we are and how to make the world a better place. You can start with a book or podcast on the topic. Or you can hire a human (like I did) to interview you and then share your best fit type (and what that means) with you. Do *something* but not *everything.*

Make a list of other different forms of art that fill your soul. Then take regular art dates to nourish your creative energy. Here are some ideas:

- Go to an art gallery or museum and take in the artwork.
- Attend a concert and soak up the music.
- Scroll Pinterest and savor all of your favorite images or ideas.
- Go for a nature walk or run and notice the natural beauty of creation.
- Take a bath while listening to your favorite playlist.
- Put your hands in clay and play (with no agenda for the end product).
- Enjoy a ballet or live stage performance of some kind.
- Take a class in a form of art that makes you happy.
- Dance like no one is watching (or watch others dance).
- Drive around your city and notice the street art or murals. Cities like New York City and London are known for their graffiti as *art.* Take notice of what's in *your* own city.
- Take a walk in your downtown and appreciate the architecture. What makes it unique from other places?
- Laugh with a comedian.

- Marvel at a magician.
- Watch pour-painting art videos on YouTube.
- Read a novel.
- Attend a paint night (yes, you're producing but being told what to do. This can get you in touch with your creative energy without putting it in the position of creating something original).

KNOW THYSELF:

Four Tendencies

From Gretchen Rubin, author of *The Four Tendencies* and creator of the free quiz:

> We all face two kinds of expectations—outer expectations (meet work deadlines, answer a request from a friend) and inner expectations (keep a New Year's resolution, start meditating). Your response to expectations determines your "Tendency"—that is, whether you're an Upholder, Questioner, Obliger, or Rebel.
>
> Knowing your Tendency can help you set up situations in ways that make it more likely that you'll achieve your aims. You can make better decisions, meet deadlines, meet your promises to yourself, suffer less stress, and engage more deeply with others.[1]

CliftonStrengths™

From my dear friend and highly gifted Certified Martha Beck Life Coach & CliftonStrengths™ Educator, Alyson Brewer:

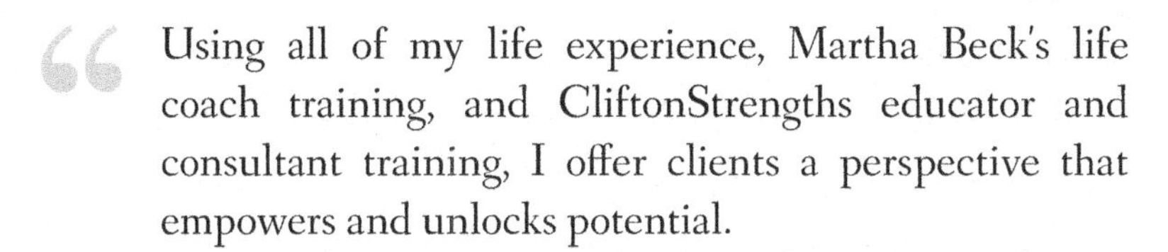

> Using all of my life experience, Martha Beck's life coach training, and CliftonStrengths educator and consultant training, I offer clients a perspective that empowers and unlocks potential.
>
> Armed with new insights, organizations and individuals are enabled to connect with each other and the world to create meaning and financial success. Sometimes all it takes is an outside perspective, small shifts in mindset, and helpful tools to bring about lasting change leading to greater performance and joy.
>
> The CliftonStrengths assessment by Gallup Inc. is a powerful tool revealing your talents and greatest potential. When understood and developed, these talents become ***strengths.***[2]

You can learn more about Alyson's work and schedule a call on her website: alysonbrewerconsulting.com/book

MBTI®

Based on one of the most influential psychologists of all time, Carl Jung, who founded analytical psychology, the Myers-Briggs Type Indicator is a widely used psychological assessment. Isabel Briggs Myers and her mother, Katharine Briggs, took Jung's theory of personality types and worked to make it accessible to the everyday person.

The Myers-Briggs Company's official website says:

> The MBTI® assessment builds an understanding of strengths and blind spots. It also helps people understand how they might differ from one another. It is valuable for individuals and teams as they tackle such

challenges as communication, handling conflict, managing change, making decisions, being a leader, or changing careers.

The MBTI® assessment is far more than just a personality questionnaire. Its benefits include:

*A common language for understanding and describing the interpersonal differences that define us as individuals

*An easy-to-understand but sophisticated way of understanding how people are similar and how they are different

*Memorable and inspiring insights that help people understand challenging relationships

*A positive view of all personalities, which avoids defensiveness and invites people to make genuine and lasting changes to their behavior

*The MBTI framework is designed specifically for individual growth and development. As such, the assessment and interpretation process provides an opportunity for personal exploration that is difficult to achieve with other assessments.

While there are online assessments that claim to be MBTI assessments, the only *actual* assessment is purchased through a certified MBTI Practitioner. My favorite way, however, is to hire a profiler, someone to interview you and walk you through your best-fit type. I've done both and found that having a human to guide me through my "it depends" responses was worth the extra cost.

One of my favorite humans on the planet, Gary Williams, is certified in and offers both the formal written assessment and profiling sessions. You can learn more about him and schedule a free discovery session through his website: betterfuturecoaching.com/links

Gary also offers support, community, education, and coaching through his **Changemaker Community**, which I mentioned in *Scarcity Blocks*. I've been in this community for over a year and love it because it lets me take what I've learned about my type and *continue growing*. This is a personal development accelerator for people who want to make a difference from *all* walks of life. Learn more or join us here: betterfuturecoaching.com/community

Enneagram

According to Truity,

> The Enneagram is a system of personality which describes people in terms of nine types, each with their own motivations, fears, and internal dynamics.
>
> The Enneagram is an emotionally focused system of understanding people — honing in on one's core emotional motivations and fears. Each of the nine personality types has its own driving force, which is centered around a particular emotion.[3]

You can hire an Enneagram profiler or take a variety of online assessments to determine your best-fit Enneagram type. Ian Cronn, a leader in all things Enneagram, offers the iEQ9, a comprehensive Ennegream assessment and report, on his website at www.ianmorgancron.com

ATTENTIONAL BLOCKS

Set your Do Not Disturb before you start writing. You can also just turn off the wi-fi or data. That'll do it too!

Put a door hanger on the door. If that doesn't work, *lock* the door. If *that* doesn't work, leave the house. Train your housemates to recognize the door hanger and respect it.

Schedule time for loved ones *and* schedule time for your book. That way you don't feel bad for doing the one when you're not doing the other.

If you have to work in a busy place, like a cafe or, ahem, a mall... bring headphones. This can help you keep focus but also communicates to those around you that you're not available for conversation.

If you need to research information in order to move forward, you can leave a note to yourself like "Add statistic/quote/fact here" and keep writing. If the information you need to find impacts your ability to move forward, then set a timer for ten or fifteen minutes and research your heart out. Then get back to writing.

When you stop writing for the day, stop in a place where you know EXACTLY what's coming next. This will give a focal point for your attention the next time you start writing again.

Trick your brain into focusing. Free write about something you like (aka a current interest) and just write something small about it. It doesn't have to be amazing or anything you'll use, just bring your attention to something you enjoy and write! This will get your brain to join you in the writing experience. Once you're locked in, segue to writing your book.

If you get bit by the "New Idea Syndrome" it's time to pull out a sheet of paper and take notes. Give your brain the satisfaction of writing it down for safekeeping (who knows, maybe it's your next bestseller?) But *keep writing.*

PROCEDURAL BLOCKS

Do *not* waste energy being upset about delays. Trust the timing, even when it veers from the plan you had. Of course, aim for your deadlines! But allow flexibility when they shift.

Pro Tips for Habits

- **Create Associations**—Choose a few things you can use to dangle in front of your brain to say, "Hey, Brain! It's writing time!" Create distinctions for your brain of writing/creating time from any other time. This might be a candle you only light when you're writing, a drink you have, a playlist you listen to, a place you sit, etc. The possibilities are endless.
- **Habit Swapping**—Trade a poor habit for something better. This means intentionally choosing to replace one thing you're doing with something better. When paired with your other ongoing associations, this is a great way to change habits.
- **Habit Stacking**—Take a habit you already have, any habit, and attach your new habit to it. There are a bunch of things you do every day without thinking about it, like taking a shower, brushing your teeth, making coffee, going for a run, getting into bed, checking the mirror, or whatever! Take that no-brainer habit and attach your new habit to it. James Clear[4] lays out the Habit Stacking formula like this: *After/Before* [*CURRENT HABIT*], *I will* [*NEW HABIT*]. After I shower, I will write for thirty minutes. After I make my Chai Latte, I will write one thousand words. After I take my kids to school, I will free write until lunch. Choose your old habit and your new habit, and get stacking!

- **Habit Pairing**—This is similar to habit stacking, except instead of one following the other, you can combine them or use one as the reward. This might be using a regular commute you have to speak and record the next part of your book (which you can have transcribed later) or treating yourself to your tradition of drinking your favorite evening tea *after* you've gotten some writing time in. What are some regular habits you have that you can pair with a new writing habit?

Pro Tips for Systems

- **Where to write the book**—Stick with what already works for you or is simple yet effective. Consider using Microsoft Word, Pages, or Google Docs for both simplicity and effectiveness. If you're not a beginner and want an overwhelming amount of versatility, consider Scrivener. Otherwise, don't overthink this—just write.
- **Speak to Text**—Don't love writing? Speak your book! Most word processors now have an accessibility option for that. On Pages, it's under "Start Dictation" (as of this writing). You can speak to your computer, and it will write the words down for you without you having to type them. You can do the same in Word with the "Dictate" feature. In Google Docs, the feature is called "Voice Typing." You can also record a voice note on your device and submit it to a platform like Otter.ai.
- **Tracked Changes**—Tracked changes is a feature in all of the word processors that allows the editor to show you (the author) what changes have been made. The changes show up in a different color. In Google Docs, this is called "Suggesting" versus "Tracked Changes." Your job is to

resolve the changes by choosing to accept or reject the change. If you reject the change, it's undone. If you accept it, it releases the "hold" on it as a suggestion and includes the edit. Now, when it's time for *you* to make changes, it's important to keep the tracked changes *on*. This allows your editor to see what you've added and changed so they can pay special attention to the new pieces you've adjusted.

Pro Tips for Workflow

- **Touch your book every day**—Even if it's just opening your manuscript and re-reading what you wrote last and adding one sentence. This keeps you connected.
- **Stay Present**—Much of our overwhelm comes from jumping into the future and imagining the *what-ifs*, and there are many! Keep track of your thoughts as they venture away from what you're working on, and bring them back to *now*.
- **Take breaks**—Breaks allow your brain to revitalize.
- Studies have shown that for about every twenty to thirty minutes of focused *learning*, you should take a three- to five-minute brain break. Find *your* best flow for writing and give yourself timed breaks.
- **What's your plan?**—Your plan won't look like my plan, and it shouldn't. The important thing is that you know the map of your process or workflow and follow it.
- **Brain dumps**—Whenever I'm stuck on a chapter (or paragraph or pothole), I'll dump all the contents of my brain on a whiteboard. This a) communicates to my brain that I'm listening b) clears up some space for creativity and c) reveals gems that were tucked away and needed an opportunity to become visible. Sometimes a to-do list or grocery list comes

out, sometimes it's processing how my life is going, and other times it's more goodies I can give my reader. In every case, I've freed myself to keep writing.

- **Permit yourself to do *you***—Take any advice in this book (or any book, article, TED talk, webinar, guru, etc.) and ditch what doesn't work for *you*. Take what partially works and mold it into something that supports you. If something works, then hold it, love it, take care of it, and write your beautiful heart out.

If you'd like help working through your procedural blocks, consider hiring someone to support you. Not only is Gary Williams my purpose and personality coach, but he's my business and mindset coach as well. Yep, he's one of those life-changers who excels in multiple crucial areas of life *and* loves helping others with his gifts and skillset.

He has several free guides as well as VIP Power Hours and workdays available on his website, betterfuturecoaching.com/links. If you're not sure what you need, consider his free Discovery Consultation call. You're already benefiting from his influence (i.e. this book).

For more tips, join me at The Writer's Block where I regularly share ways to overcome writer's block to beat the blank page! You can join us here: miramarepontepress.com/thewritersblock

notes

2. WHAT CAUSES WRITER'S BLOCK?

1. Team, G. T. E. (2019, November 1). *Creative blocks.* GoodTherapy. Retrieved September 9, 2022, from https://www.goodtherapy.org/learn-about-therapy/issues/creative-blocks.

3. MENTAL BLOCKS

1. Duran, A. (2022, July 29). *What is a mental block: Overcoming mental blocks.* Sage Neuroscience Center. Retrieved September 9, 2022, from https://sageclinic.org/blog/overcoming-mental-blocks/
2. Bohn, R., and Short, J. 2012. *Measuring consumer information.* Int. J. Comm. 6:980–1000.
3. Heim, S., & Keil, A. (2017, June 1). *Too much information, too little time: How the brain separates important from unimportant things in our fast-paced media world.* Frontiers for Young Minds. Retrieved September 9, 2022, from https://kids.frontiersin.org/articles/10.3389/frym.2017.00023

5. MENTAL BLOCKS

1. Tseng, J., & Poppenk, J. (2020, July 13). *Brain Meta-state transitions demarcate thoughts across task contexts exposing the mental noise of trait neuroticism.* Nature News. Retrieved September 9, 2022, from https://rdcu.be/cVi7g
2. LifeXchange. (n.d.). *Did you know this part of the brain drives all your teams' behaviour & performance?* Your Brain at Work: The Reticular Activating System (RAS) and Your Goals & Behaviour. Retrieved September 10, 2022, from https://lifexchangesolutions.com/reticular-activating-system/
3. Stone, J. (2014, November 19). *The 7 laws of impatience.* Psychology Today. Retrieved October 15, 2022, from https://www.psychologytoday.com/us/blog/clear-organized-and-motivated/201411/the-7-laws-impatience

15. SCARCITY BLOCKS

1. Rubin, G. (n.d.). *Getting started: The Four Tendencies.* Gretchen Rubin. Retrieved October 23, 2022, from https://gretchenrubin.com/four-tendencies/

18. ATTENTIONAL BLOCKS

1. Aronson, S. (2019, September 23). *Divided attention and the search for self.* Gurdjieff Club. Retrieved September 22, 2022, from https://gurdjieffclub.com/en/divided_attention_and_the_search_for_self_882/
2. Dehaene, S. (2020, September 30). *How we pay attention changes the very shape of our brains.* Literary Hub. Retrieved September 21, 2022, from https://lithub.com/how-we-pay-attention-changes-the-very-shape-of-our-brains/:~:text=The%20neurons%20that%20encode%20the,the%20rest%20of%20the%20brain.

20. ATTENTIONAL BLOCKS

1. Saad, S. K. (2019, November 15). *What happens to your brain when you get a phone notification.* Bustle. Retrieved September 21, 2022, from https://www.bustle.com/p/what-happens-to-your-brain-when-you-get-a-phone-notification-19256076

21. ATTENTIONAL BLOCKS

1. Aronson, S. (2019, September 23). *Divided attention and the search for self.* Gurdjieff Club. Retrieved September 22, 2022, from https://gurdjieffclub.com/en/divided_attention_and_the_search_for_self_882/

23. PROCEDURAL BLOCKS

1. McLachlan, S. (2021, December 22). *The Science of Habit: How to Rewire Your Brain.* Healthline. Retrieved October 15, 2022, from https://www.healthline.com/health/the-science-of-habit#2

26. PROCEDURAL BLOCKS

1. Clear, J. (2020, February 4). *How to build new habits by taking advantage of Old ones.* James Clear. Retrieved September 23, 2022, from https://jamesclear.com/habit-stacking
2. Clear, J. (2020, February 4). *How to build new habits by taking advantage of Old ones.* James Clear. Retrieved October 15, 2022, from https://jamesclear.com/habit-stacking
3. Willis, J. (2018). *Resetting the mind to focus: The science of a brain break.* AddyPres LifeSTYLE. Retrieved September 23, 2022, from https://addypreslifestyle.com/resetting-the-mind-to-focus-the-science-of-a-brain-break/

PRO TIPS

1. Rubin, G. (n.d.). *Getting started: The Four Tendencies.* Gretchen Rubin. Retrieved October 23, 2022, from https://gretchenrubin.com/four-tendencies/
2. *Elevating teams,empowering individuals, engineering transformation.* Alyson Brewer Consulting. (n.d.). Retrieved October 23, 2022, from https://alysonbrewerconsulting.com/
3. *What are the nine enneagram types?* Truity. (2021, November 5). Retrieved October 23, 2022, from https://www.truity.com/enneagram/9-types-enneagram
4. Clear, J. (2020, February 4). *How to build new habits by taking advantage of Old ones.* James Clear. Retrieved September 23, 2022, from https://jamesclear.com/habit-stacking

Made in the USA
Columbia, SC
05 February 2024